MW00973880

# BALANCING
# WORK
## AND
# FAMILY

## The WorkSmart Series

# BALANCING WORK AND FAMILY

## Ken Lizotte
## Barbara A. Litwak

### amacom
AMERICAN MANAGEMENT ASSOCIATION
THE WORKSMART SERIES

New York • Atlanta • Boston • Chicago • Kansas City • San Francisco • Washington, D.C.
Brussels • Toronto • Mexico City

*This book is available at a special*
*discount when ordered in bulk quantities.*
*For information, contact Special Sales Department,*
*AMACOM, a division of American Management Association,*
*135 West 50th Street, New York, NY 10020.*

*This publication is designed to provide accurate and authoritative information in regard to the subject matter covered. It is sold with the understanding that the publisher is not engaged in rendering legal, accounting, or other professional service. If legal advice or other expert assistance is required, the services of a competent professional person should be sought.*

*Library of Congress Cataloging-in-Publication Data*

*Lizotte, Ken.*
    *Balancing work and family / Ken Lizotte, Barbara A. Litwak.*
            *p.   cm.—(The workSmart series)*
    *Includes bibliographical references.*
    *ISBN 0-8144-7837-9*
    *1. Work and family.   I. Litwak, Barbara A.   II. Title.*
*III.  Series.*
*HD4904.25.L59    1995*
*646.7'8—dc20*                                          *95-19855*
                                                              *CIP*

*© 1995 AMACOM, a division of*
*American Management Association, New York.*
*All rights reserved.*
*Printed in the United States of America.*

*This publication may not be reproduced,*
*stored in a retrieval system,*
*or transmitted in whole or in part,*
*in any form or by any means, electronic,*
*mechanical, photocopying, recording, or otherwise,*
*without the prior written permission of AMACOM,*
*a division of American Management Association,*
*135 West 50th Street, New York, NY 10020.*

*Printing number*

*10   9   8   7   6   5   4   3   2*

To my parents,
a true balancing act.

—B.A.L.


To my brother Ed,
a truly balanced guy.

—K.L.

# CONTENTS

# CHAPTER 1

## WHAT'S BALANCE TO YOU?

It's a funny thing about life; if you refuse to accept anything but the best, you very often get it.

—Somerset Maugham, British writer

Every Monday, Wednesday, and Friday, Mary Cronin rises at 5:30 A.M. to make breakfast for her husband and three kids. Although due at her own job at 8 A.M. sharp, Mary doesn't really mind the added pressure. She knows that her husband, Bob, will be up to make breakfast on Tuesday, Thursday, and Saturday. (They alternate Sundays.) Both Mary and Bob work full-time, but they've worked out a system, just as they have for family duties in the evenings and on weekends.

Mary and Bob live active, full lives. They're successful professionals (she in sales, he in engineering) who socialize often. (He golfs every Sunday while she plays tennis at her club.) Their children are energetic and busy, and they all go off for vacations together twice a year, once in the summer and once around Christmas.

"It's not always easy trying to balance family, work, and personal time, but we've managed it," Mary says. "Our long days pay off in the end—although I'll admit it's a real juggling act."

Many people would agree with Mary's assessment: Yes, they *do* have a balanced lifestyle. With a lot of "juggling" and more than a few long, wearying days, Mary and Bob (and their children) get to do most of the things they want to do. To them, it seems worth it.

But how does Mary and Bob's life sound to *you?* If you're searching for a way to balance your own work and personal life, does their approach appeal to you? Or perhaps you wish for another way?

Rightly or wrongly, it seems that whenever people talk about how to balance work life and personal life successfully, the standard is Mary and Bob's kind of action-packed "juggling act." A now rather time-worn phrase, "having it all" exhorts us to hold down full-time, fast-track professional jobs while simultaneously raising a robust family *and* keeping marriage fun and exciting. Oh yes, and don't forget "personal" time—hobbies, sports, recreation, meditation!

But is this what most of us really want? Do we aspire to Mary and Bob's lifestyle because it truly appeals to us? Is it really all that it's cracked up to be?

## A PEEK THROUGH THE BACK DOOR

Consider a second peek at Mary and Bob, this time through the "back door." In their kitchen, late at night, we see Bob wolfing down his dinner. He's just gotten home (it's after 11 P.M.), even though he left at 7:30 this morning. Mary enters, looking pretty worn out. She tells Bob that she finally got the kids to bed.

"But I'll be up for a while," she says next, setting up a pot of coffee. "Got to prepare for my presentation tomorrow. I haven't had a minute to think about it until now."

Mary tells us later, "We're both usually pretty beat by the time we get home, but there's always plenty more to do. Laundry, dinner, cleaning. If it's my turn with the kids, or if Bob's late getting home, any work I bring home waits until the children's bedtime. The same goes for him."

**The key to a truly balanced lifestyle is not what you do on the outside but how you feel about it on the inside.**

Bob's moment of candor? "Sometimes I just wish we lived on an island somewhere, eating coconuts and frolicking on the beach. Sometimes I just wish it were simpler."

Although having it all and doing it all may be a perfectly valid form of achieving a balanced lifestyle, we want Bob to know that it *could* be simpler! The key to a truly balanced lifestyle is not what you do on the outside but how you feel about it on the inside. That's in contrast with popular notions of a "balanced life" defined as a wide variety of external activities, all somehow perfectly juggled against one another. You may find yourself trying to live up to such images as the "superwoman" or the "perfect man" or some other idealized media fantasy. This is great for splashy book or magazine ideas, but it's darn hard for you and me to live up to.

Could Mary and Bob be trying to live up to such media standards, copying fictional views of the balanced lifestyle, living life the way they suppose they *should*, not the way they'd really want to? Have they taken time to carve out a personal perspective on what a balanced lifestyle really means? Have they formally written out their Personal Balance Statements? Most people never do.

People truly achieve balance only when they choose to live the way they want. They feel in balance when they sense a centeredness, when they're inwardly confident about what they're doing. Each of us is a unique combination of emotions, thoughts, ideas, abilities, memories, desires. What balances one of us won't necessarily balance the other. I love classical music, you love good old rock and roll. I love peach melba, you adore strawberry rhubarb pie. I relax by reading *Scientific American,* you by competing in Monster Tractor Trailer Rallies.

## SETTING YOUR OWN STANDARDS

Although this seems obvious—that we're all so different—we often spend our lives reaching for someone else's brass ring or trying to emulate a lifestyle that seems as if it should be fulfilling, yet never quite satisfies us. For example:

- The attorney who hates law but couldn't bear to disappoint his lawyer-father and lawyer-grandfather by dropping his practice. He certainly couldn't tell them that he longed instead to be a pro golfer!
- The mother of six who feels she doesn't really work for a living. Although her husband supports her in her choice to stay home and raise their family, she compares herself constantly to working women she sees on talk shows who boast about "having it all."
- The twentysomething single professional who worries about her one-dimensional life. Although she loves her work, loves the travel it demands, and loves the satisfaction of a project well done, she quietly berates herself for not socializing more, not finding a mate, not getting married, not settling down and raising a family. Simply working hard and loving it isn't good enough.
- The married couple who so love spending time with each other that they don't seem to want any children. Yet both their mothers keep pushing the question: "Sooo . . . when are you going to make me a grandmother? Hmmm?" The couple keeps asking each other what's wrong with them.

**Stop listening to everybody but yourself! You will create true balance in your life only by setting your own standards and fashioning your own definition of balance.**

Did you see yourself in any of these scenarios? Or perhaps you've got one of your own! If you want to define the balance in your life that's right for you, you must first take one critical and difficult step: *Stop listening to everybody but yourself!* You will create true balance in your life only by setting your own standards and fashioning your own definition of balance. You need to decide what personally makes you feel that life is worthwhile.

Need some examples? Here are a few Personal Balance Statements from people we've known to get you thinking about how to define your own. Remember, these are other people's definitions of balance, not yours. They might appeal to you or inspire you, but you will still want to fashion one that's unique to you.

### Personal Balance Statements

My vision of a balanced life is one in which I have a few really good friends, not a large entourage.

My vision of personal balance is to work part-time and take care of my family the rest of the time.

I want a life in which I have lots of friends, do lots of socializing, and am busy all the time.

Give me a life that permits me to grow—plenty of reading, thinking, intellectualizing with colleagues!

I envision a life in which I achieve great things in my work but also maintain a happy and loving family life.

A Personal Balance Statement can be very simple, or it can be more complicated with two or more ideas sewn together. We suggest, though, that you keep your Personal Balance Statement fairly simple, at least at first. Your Personal Balance Statement should frame your life, not outline it in detail. Details are the goals, directions, specific steps that you need to take to achieve your Personal Balance. The vision itself must be flexible enough to allow for surprises, obstacles, and opportunities along the way.

## YOUR PERSONAL BALANCE

Let's try now to define your Personal Balance. If you have trouble, don't worry: We'll be engaging in other exercises to help flesh it out. You can always come back and revise or replace your Personal Balance Statement at any time. Right now we just want to see what comes up spontaneously in a preliminary self-examination.

Start with "I want a life in which . . ." or "My definition of Personal Balance is to . . ." Use the space below for your

Personal Balance Statement. If you have trouble putting it into words, use as much paper as you like to sketch out your feelings or doodle some kind of illustration of what you feel. Exercises throughout this book will help you flesh out the definition of your Personal Balance further. Note: We suggest that, to realize the full impact of this exercise and some of the others in this book, you pick up a package of magic markers or borrow a few of your children's crayons (just a few—your kids need them too!). By using color you'll access more segments of your brain and thus more aspects of yourself. This could result in a truer, more rounded picture of who you are.

# PERSONAL BALANCE STATEMENT

Now let's get a little more specific about what would make your life more balanced. In the accompanying Want Box, allow yourself to imagine, speculate, fantasize, dream. Put down anything you can think of that would make your life fulfilling, worthwhile, exhilarating, or fun. Just fill up the space inside the box and keep listing things until you can't think of anything more. Do not censor yourself! This is your chance to get really close to the heart of your Personal Balance Statement.

## WANT BOX

Fill up the space inside this box with as many personal aspirations in your life as you can think of. Include goals and ambitions from all categories—career, family, friends, social life, spiritual growth, recreation, health. Maybe you can think of other categories. Your mission here is to flesh out your Personal Balance Statement by getting more detailed about how you want your life to be.

Have you completed your Want Box? Great! Now go on to the Priority Pie Chart below. Illustrate in this pie chart your ideal of a balanced lifestyle by carving out wedges proportional to the priority you place upon each category of your life. Once again, wedges may include career, family, friends, recreation, spiritual growth, health, and whatever other categories you like. Include subitems in each wedge that elaborate upon each priority. Example: Subitems for "many good friends" might include "trusting, fun-loving, great dancers, movie-lovers, parties once a month, spontaneous."

Now compare your priorities with the way you currently direct your efforts and time. What do you need to work on to make your present life more consistent with your priorities? Make a list of action steps you will take to get yourself closer to a balanced lifestyle.

| | **Action Steps** | **Priorities Served** |
|---|---|---|
| 1. | _____ | _____ |
| 2. | _____ | _____ |
| 3. | _____ | _____ |
| 4. | _____ | _____ |
| 5. | _____ | _____ |
| 6. | _____ | _____ |
| 7. | _____ | _____ |
| 8. | _____ | _____ |
| 9. | _____ | _____ |
| 10. | _____ | _____ |

Now revise or replace your Personal Balance Statement as your Priority Pie Chart implies. What elements did you originally include because you thought you should? What elements did you leave out because you hadn't considered how much they really mean to you? Once you have finished, insert your revised Personal Balance Statement in the space below. (Again, use more paper if you want to.) Remember, flexibility will be your ally throughout this process. If you allow yourself to keep rethinking how to best define your Personal Balance, you will keep it fresh and vibrant, and strong enough to overcome obstacles and changing conditions.

# REVISED PERSONAL BALANCE STATEMENT

# CHAPTER 2

## BREAKING THROUGH YOUR BLOCKS

A problem is a chance for you to do your best.

—Duke Ellington, American jazz
composer and performer

When confronted with a block, most people's first impulse is to submit to it. Facing blocks can be overwhelming, as in "What do I do now? How will I ever deal with this one?" Your brain goes numb; no clear direction or strategy comes immediately to mind.

That's just a natural response, of course, designed to create time to process the problem and organize your thoughts toward a solution. The key is not to panic and give up. Instead, be patient and let yourself speculate, ruminate, ponder, muse. You are working on your problem. Ultimately, your block is your belief that you may never find a solution. It's rarely something external.

Suppose your Personal Balance Statement reads, "I want to have a wonderful married life and a fabulous family." Initially, your brain blocks you from knowing how to achieve this. Internally, you may even say, "Nice idea, but I don't even have a significant other, let alone a budding family."

First, be patient. Relax. Sit back in a soft chair. Take a load off. Breathe in slowly, then breathe out. Let thoughts or ideas roam freely in your mind and don't worry if they're not practical enough, or whether they're reasonable or logical or "implementable." Begin jotting down notes of whatever comes into your mind, and watch your ideas flow: blind dates, parties, joining a singles club. Some ideas might be downright wacky: interview potential mates in a supermarket, order your future spouse from a catalog, build a mate out of holograms. Write them down! As your ideas flow, strategies emerge. You are moving toward an answer.

Involve friends or colleagues in the process, and watch your ideas and potential solutions mushroom! Just be sure your friends and colleagues are positive. Make certain you and they allow *any* idea to emerge. Idea, idea, idea, bing, bing, bing! Traditionally this has been called brainstorming, though we like the more modern term "freewheeling." Be free, wheel your imagination around. Don't worry about the practicality of your ideas; just keep them flowing. Blocks hold you back, while generating positive ideas gets you moving.

You can always do something about your blocks, no matter how daunting. Not a penny to your name? Find a job, start a business, borrow money from a friend, panhandle on the street. Out of shape, low energy, always tired? See a doctor, join a gym, take vitamins, eat better, get more sleep. Can't stand your job? Children won't behave? There are always answers. (Yes, parents, for you too!) The decision that there aren't, or that you've already thought of everything, is just an excuse to quit looking.

**Once you've identified what you don't have but wish you did, you acquire self-knowledge about what you want and how to get it.**

## BLOCK PORTRAIT

When you use your blocks in this way—clinging to them, refusing to initiate a blockbusting technique like freewheeling—you create excuses. But when you use your blocks to take you to a next step, they'll point you in a new direction and tell you what's missing. Once you've identified what you don't have but wish you did, you acquire self-knowledge about what you want and how to get it.

So to effectively break through your blocks, first define them. In the space below, draw a picture of yourself with your blocks all around you. Show in your drawing how your blocks exert power over you. (What? You say you can't draw? You haven't picked up a box of crayons since first grade and you sure don't want to go back to picking any up right now? Good work! You've just defined another block. Dust yourself off, tear into those magic markers, and have fun busting through this too, your most up-to-the-minute block!)

## MY BLOCK PORTRAIT

## BLOCK WHEEL

Now let's connect your blocks to ideas that could lead to solutions. In each space of the wheel below, write in the name of one of your blocks. Outside the wheel, jot down ideas for breaking through them. Use as much space outside the wheel as you like. If you need to, draw a similar wheel on a larger sheet of paper.

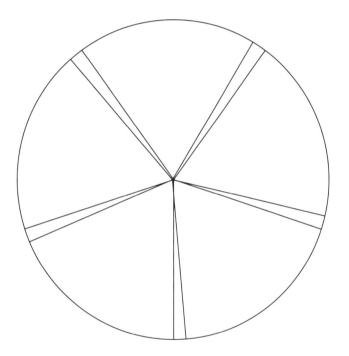

Blocks of some kind will always be with you. Besides, if people didn't have problems and blocks, how would they learn, grow, achieve? Like it or not, life would get pretty boring. In many ways, dealing with blocks is really what life is all about. So always see your blocks as signposts for moving forward while you freewheel, freewheel down the road.

### The Freewheeling Process

- Relax, settle your mind, and breathe slowly.
- Let ideas, thoughts, and pictures float freely into your mind.

- Jot down notes of as many ideas, thoughts, and mental pictures as you can.
- Do not censor yourself. Weed out impractical ideas later.
- After at least ten to fifteen minutes, take a break, and then come back for a fresh look at your list.
- Circle all ideas you find intriguing.
- Next circle all the ideas you'd like to implement or explore further.
- Make a separate list of the ideas you've circled. What action steps can you take to bring them to life?
- List all your action steps, then set a time frame for implementing them.
- Begin taking action, and watch your blocks melt away!

**You *can* break through any block, no matter how challenging. To believe otherwise, as we have said, is to harbor an excuse to not try.**

## BLOCKBUSTING MADE EASY

Once you are able to define what your blocks are, breaking them becomes simply a matter of faith and positive thinking. You *can* break through any block, no matter how challenging. To believe otherwise, as we have said, is to harbor an excuse to not try.

We favor a simple three-step method for breaking through your blocks. Although simple may not always mean easy—some blocks are tougher to break than others—this process will get you started (often the hardest part) and move you toward victory.

Our three-step process for breaking blocks goes like this:

### Step 1: Believe You Can!

Sounds Pollyanna-ish, Norman Vincent Peale-ish, Forrest Gump-ish, we know, but you've really got to start with this one. Try *not* believing you can break through your blocks and see how far you get. Dr. Charles Garfield, a motivation

**Dr. Charles Garfield, a motivation expert and author of a study on peak performers, says that the greatest single characteristic of those who achieve their goals is the simple "belief that you can do it."**

expert and author of a study on peak performers, says that the greatest single characteristic of those who achieve their goals is the simple "belief that you can do it." Not education, not gender, not age, not strength, not intelligence, not contacts nor anything else, Garfield proclaims. His voluminous research on peak performers is clear: Believing in yourself is paramount.

The terrible anxieties and self-doubt that infect people, the sheer terror of facing some of their blocks, and a deep confusion about which strategy to employ frequently hold people back from giving their blockbreaking efforts the requisite "old college try." So commit yourself to doing whatever you have to by believing in your capacity to follow through successfully. Although you may be clueless about how you will eventually pull it off, you cannot begin this process in an optimal way without believing you can win.

## Step 2: Imagine Yourself Doing It!

Even when you find yourself in mortal fear of your block, you still have the power to imagine what life would be like without it. Fantasize that this block is no longer in your life, that you've gained dominion over it. *Wow!* Just imagine! What would things be like otherwise? What would *you* be like?

Suppose you're scared to death of public speaking. (Surveys show, in fact, that more people fear public speaking than death, anyway!) You want to do something about it; you feel that public speaking skills would advance you professionally and help you grow personally. You've decided that you can overcome your fears (step 1 accomplished!) but now you've got to figure out *how.*

Relax in a soft chair or on a couch or sit by a bubbly brook or in your garden. Have a cup of tea with you or a bottle of water, something restful (no drugs or alcohol). Breathe in slowly, breathe out. Take in your surroundings. Let image-float into your mind, then float away. Quiet yourself.

Now, observe yourself striding confidently into a Toastmasters' Club meeting at your local library. You shake hands with everyone and smile and take in the camaraderie. Yes, you're a little nervous, that's natural, but you're glad to be there.

You watch yourself volunteer to be the first speaker, then smoothly execute your speech. Gracefully you accept feedback from your attentive, discerning audience, listening carefully to all comments. This feedback is good; it will help you get better at this. You love being here! You're a public speaker!

That's all you need to do in step 2—welcome pictures and images into your head, observe yourself acting and living a life you *want*. See yourself handling the gritty details. Hey, the best thing here is that this doesn't cost you anything, and on top of that nobody can tell you that you didn't do it right! Have some fun! Don't worry about a thing. Just imagine yourself handling this in a completely different way!

## Step 3: Act as if You've Already Done It!

Susan Jeffers titled her book about breaking through fears (blocks) this way: *Feel the Fear and Do It Anyway*. The title truly says it all.

Return to our previous example of public speaking. Now it's time to physically *go* to a Toastmasters' Club meeting. You've imagined doing it, but you can't deny that you're still more than a little shaky about it.

While imagining yourself doing this, you sketched out a script to follow. That directs your brain to coordinate your behavior in a particular way. So you drive to the library on the appointed evening and bravely push yourself through the door of the Toastmasters' Club meeting room. Despite how you feel inside ("Whoever's knees are rattling, would they please stop?"), you try playing the part of a cool, calm, and collected novice speaker. You're not trying to put on airs here; you just want to convey that you know you can do this and that your nervousness will not defeat you. You're up to the challenge. You're in the right room.

If you keep thinking this way, behaving as though you are more confident than you in fact really feel, one night (maybe the first night!) you'll surprise yourself as you notice how confident you've become. You'll be excited to be there and you'll actually be looking forward to stepping up to the podium (though probably still a little nervous). Somewhere along the way you'll have stopped being terrified.

You'll officially be a public speaker and your block will be gone!

## BALANCING ACT: ALICE HALE

For more than twenty years, Alice Hale had felt completely secure in her career. A high school history teacher, she'd been appointed head of the department at age 22, an event that would set the tone of her work and life for two decades. She could ignore recessions and job market turmoil and just go to work and do her job. As a divorced single mother, she could raise her son, Tim, and never worry about the outside world.

But after she passed age 40, Alice's life changed. The cutbacks and layoffs and downsizings she'd been dimly hearing about, stories of work and family lives getting torn apart in private industry throughout the 1980s, suddenly came slashing her way. Her town's school board began chopping up its budget and eliminating entire departments. Once sacred cows, these departments had now been rendered obsolete, untenable, a luxury. She got word about her own dismissal from the newspapers: Her safe, secure, comfortable, familiar routine would be over at the end of June.

"I have no connections, I'm too old, I'm not qualified for anything else," she told anyone who would listen. She felt her life beginning to unravel. "I only know teaching. What will I do? What? I'm just terrified!"

Alice worried about other blocks, too, great, lurking internal ones. As she considered moving herself from here to there, she confronted a truth about herself.

"I'm a classic self–saboteur," she confided to us. "Whenever I try to change my life I make sure I don't succeed. I'll do everything I'm supposed to, everything people say you've got to do to make progress, but I keep resisting the process all the way. I refuse to let myself succeed."

### Balance Check

- If your own work life faced a sudden end or radical change, how would you react? Would you share Alice's panic? What personal blocks of yours might contribute to your fears?
- What's your vision of where you'd like to go, whether your current work life continues or not? Refer to your Personal Balance Statement.
- What course of action might you follow to solve a crisis such as Alice encountered? Do you have any specific action steps in mind?
- How might you have advised Alice had she brought her fears and concerns to you?

In the midst of this crisis Alice surprised herself. With our guidance, she began by "de-whelming" herself, breaking down the scary big picture she faced, downsizing it into small, realizable steps. That got her started. With each step she advanced a little further down the path. And each time she stepped off, she automatically left an old place and arrived somewhere new—new vistas, new resources, fresh possibilities.

By taking such beginning steps, Alice got herself into gear, despite her terror. What form did her steps take? She simply began chatting with people. That was all at first, just chatting folks up. Here's my story, sad but true. Everyone she met got an earful—grocers, mailmen, gas station attendants, old friends. Astonishingly, the mere act of reporting her personal crisis to others released many of her blocks. People returned positive feedback to her about all her concerns.

"I'm trying to find out what I want to do next, but I'm not sure what that is," she told anyone and everyone who would listen. "I'm looking for a new opportunity." Alice's openings were short, sweet, and candid. Now lob the ball back.

### Balance Check

- If Alice had approached you, how would you have lobbed her ball back? What advice or suggestions might you have given her?
- Would you be able to carry out Alice's plan of action? What blocks might get in your way? What are some ideas for breaking through these blocks?
- Can you imagine another course of action for breaking this crisis down into manageable steps? What personal blocks might get in your way?

Nearly all the people Alice talked to had some kind of idea, suggestion, or tale of their own life turnarounds to offer her. Many truly great conversations ensued, including not a few invaluable ideas from totally unexpected sources. Soon she had so many options to explore there was no time left for panic, self-denigration, or hopelessness. She could make this change, whatever it was going to be. She really could.

All these interactions, all this chit-chat with a purpose, propelled Alice Hale into a new image of herself and of what life could be. She put all the pieces together, including her home life with her son, Tim. She could spend more time with him, help him grow, pay attention. She could feel more creative and confident and personally powerful than she'd ever felt working at the school.

Someone somewhere told her about a man who wanted to sell a profitable home-based newsletter. After speaking with others who ran similar businesses, Alice quickly came to understand, to her amazement, how eminently qualified she was: Her excellent organizing and editing skills would enable her to set up the business easily in her own home, and she also began noticing a knack for coming up with creative ideas for better marketing the business. The ideas just started flowing through her head and she couldn't stop them. The more she thought of herself in this new role, in fact, the more she felt that she could manage this business even better than its present owner!

So she took out a second mortgage on her home, negotiated a fair price for all, and bought herself a new world.

"I'm independent now, in control of my life," she could later report to all those willing contacts and resources she'd met along the way. "Now no one can fire me—I'm running my own show. That forces me to be more creative, energized, and alive than I ever was at the school! It's up to *me* to keep making things happen now. That's still a scary thought at times, but not so scary as the idea that I couldn't make my life work out the way I want to."

### Balance Check

- Could you have taken the risk Alice took? Would a home-based business appeal to you? What positive attributes and talents could you bring to such a work life?
- If a home-based business does not appeal to you, what opportunity would you rather have stumbled upon? What talents and skills could you bring to such an opportunity?
- Are there any particular aspects of your home life or your personal goals that might be affected by a work-change crisis such as this one? How could your personal life and goals be advanced positively by such a crisis? What blocks would get in the way of your turning this crisis into an opportunity for healthy growth?

As so often transpires when people break through blocks and start taking command of their lives, Alice's universe turned around completely as a result of her decisions. In the midst of all this remarkable personal change, in fact, her school reinstated her department and offered her her old job back. Immediately she thought, "How dare they! They just got me used to the idea that they don't want me anymore, and

I finally came to accept that. Now they want to drag me back. The arrogance!" My, how the lady had changed!

But Alice reframed the dilemma as a window of opportunity, a challenge to her new assertiveness. What if she could shape this into something that worked for her? Sure, I'll come back, she decided to tell the school principal, but first I want you to release my accumulated retirement funds to me, then hire me on a part-time basis only, and at hours of my own choosing. The old Alice would never have even thought of doing this.

So Alice Hale now works mornings as a teacher, the profession she carefully crafted throughout most of her adult life, and the rest of her day as a successful desktop publisher. She spends much time with her son, takes classes in areas of other interest, and runs her own life.

Do blocks and old doubts still rumble around in her head, taunting her, pushing at her? Sure, they keep trying to creep back in, she acknowledges, but they're no longer welcome, nor do they visit for very long. Whatever blocks come her way now, whatever terrors spring forward, she faces them down. She's worked out her own definition of balance, and she's made it reality.

### Balance Check

- How prepared are you for a similar crisis in your work life? What action steps must you take to be fully prepared? What personal blocks hold you back from getting fully prepared?
- What if a similar crisis hit your home life? Do you do all you can to prevent it? Do you give full attention to your loved ones, keeping communication with them strong? Does your Personal Balance Statement reflect your desires for your personal life?
- What does our discussion of blocks imply for your overall thinking and behavior? Which blocks do you need to work on first? Which blocks can you eradicate completely? Which blocks get in your way the most?

# BLOCKS WE HAVE KNOWN AND LOVED

Whether in our own lives, in the lives of our clients, or just kicking around the universe, we've encountered many of the same blocks over and over. They're listed in the accompanying worksheet. Some of these may be one of yours at the moment. Or have you concocted a few that are unique to you? (If so, good work! Always acknowledge your creative achievements!)

## MY OWN PET BLOCKS

Please check off all blocks in the following list that you recognize as your own. Then circle the top three blocks you've checked off, those that are now holding you back the most. Finally, place a star beside the block most holding you back among your top three.

Fear of failure
Fear of success
Procrastination
Perfectionism
Low self-confidence
Negative thinking
Lack of spontaneity
Not a risk taker
Too shy
Not enough time
Not enough money
Not good-looking enough

Fear of authority
Always seeking approval
Giving up too soon
Thinking I'm not smart enough
Regretting the past
Laziness
Concoctions of my own:

_____
_____
_____
_____
_____

Once you've designated your Top Block, try out our three-step process. Then, after you've vanquished this block from your life, or while you're still chipping away at it, get started on block 2. Gradually work your way down your whole list. Note: We said gradually. Don't take on all your blocks at once!

# CHAPTER 3

## SETTING YOUR OWN AGENDA

Make big plans, aim high in hope and work.

— Daniel H. Burnham, American architect

It's easy to listen to others tell you what life is all about, isn't it? It's often *too* easy! Some people spend their whole lives doing what they think others want them to—an approach that gets things done but doesn't necessarily lead to balance unless it feels right viscerally.

Listen to yourself. Go on, listen. Define the most important activity you could be engaged in right now. What could you be doing to keep yourself on track, to advance your personal goals? What activities today would bring you closer to your definition of Personal Balance?

Make a list of everything you feel you need to do this week.

1. _____
2. _____
3. _____
4. _____
5. _____
6. _____
7. _____
8. _____

(If you need more space, use another sheet of paper.)

Now circle in red (or the color of your choice) all the items you've put on your list because you really *want* to. Also circle the items that will make you feel particularly satisfied—we'll call those "personal triumphs." Leave alone all the other items, the ones you've listed purely out of a sense of obligation, guilt, or duress.

How does your list look now? If you've circled everything in red, you're probably doing pretty well. Your life may be in a nice state of balance already. If so, reward yourself! Go have some fun! All the other well-balanced people in the world will be waiting for you at the party.

Now for the rest of us. Look over your uncircled items. Why did you list them in the first place? Why do you think you have to do them? Can you delegate some and just jettison the rest? How many could you convert to activities you'd *like* to be doing?

There are certainly duties and obligations people can't avoid. As we mentioned before, life isn't perfect. You may not enjoy some of the items on your list—"Change baby's diapers," "Have frank discussion with difficult boss," "Visit friend in the hospital"—but we'd all agree that they still have to be done.

But how about those gray areas? Why are you planning to go to that party Saturday night when you don't like parties? Why do you keep working for an employer that treats you so badly? Why stay on the phone so long with friends talking about subjects that don't interest you? Life is short, and your body clock is tick-tick-ticking away. Let's get on with it!

Setting your own agenda can be hard. It may mean that you need to learn to say "no" more. It may mean that you need to begin practicing the art of "decommitting," or disengaging from activities you now realize, in your new balanced wisdom, you don't really want to do. It may mean taking on challenges that strike you at first glance as "too hard" or even frightening but whose successful execution would mean a lot to you.

Are you active in two or more professional organizations, for example, because you feel it's "good for networking"? Maybe it is, but what can you find on your list that you'd rather be doing, that you never get to because of lack of

**Setting your own agenda can be hard. It may mean that you need to learn to say "no" more. It may mean that you need to begin practicing the art of "decommitting," or disengaging from activities you now realize, in your new balanced wisdom, you don't really want to do.**

time? Would cutting back to just one professional group free you up? How much would your networking activities suffer if you concentrated your energies in one organization rather than scattering them all over town?

Often schedules people set for themselves derive from their "block-headedness." Perhaps you let lack of confidence, for example, set the parameters of any number of items on your agenda. To gain control of your daily planning, you've got to stay focused on your Personal Balance Statement and keep choosing activities that move you in the right direction. Since this can be trickier than it sounds, ask yourself these questions when making or reviewing your to-do list:

- *Do I really want to do this?* If yes, then just do it!
- *Is this task urgent or absolutely necessary?* If yes, then do it!
- *Can I delegate this?* If yes, then do so!
- *Can I be more flexible about this, possibly put it off until another time so that I can do something I really want to do today?* If yes, then delay, delay, delay!
- *Do I really have to do this, or do I just think I have to?* If you've any doubt at all about doing something you don't want to do, analyze how you came to decide you *had* to do this thing. If you can't resolve your doubts, don't do it!
- *Can I change how I do this in the future?* If yes, change away!

## AGENDA OF DESIRE

Compose an Agenda of Desire, basically a plan of action for attaining your Personal Balance Statement. Include in your Agenda of Desire as many action steps as you can think of, and time frames and deadlines. List only those items that fit criteria established by the above questions, that is, goals that reflect your values as expressed by your Personal Balance Statement. Write your Agenda of Desire in first person, present tense, utilizing active verbs. Don't forget to include rewards to yourself. For example:

# PERSONAL BALANCE STATEMENT

I am working as vice president of sales by January 1, 1999.

## Action Steps Required:

- I am winning sales contests by March 1, 1997.
- I am exceeding all sales quota by September 1, 1997.
- I am buying myself a new car by December 15, 1997.
- I am working as sales manager by April 30, 1998.
- I am breaking all sales records for my division by September 30, 1998.
- I am treating myself to a well-deserved vacation by October 15, 1998.
- I am competing for the position of VP of sales by November 15, 1998.

# SEVEN WAYS TO "RIGHTSIZE" YOUR WORK SCHEDULE

Is your job getting in the way of your life? When you spend too much time at a job you don't like; or when your hours conflict with other aspects of your life; or when you spend too much time commuting, hanging out at the water cooler, or dealing with problem colleagues, it's time to "rightsize" your career—that is, convert to an alternative work option. Which of the following ideas might offer you greater balance between your work and family life?

## 1. Telecommuting, or Working From Home

Hopping onto the Information Highway is a burgeoning trend today, and companies as well as individual professionals love it more and more! Telecommuting cuts down on the need for office spaces for everybody, it allows for happier, more motivated workers, and it enables a company to maintain staff in other areas of the country or the world. That's invaluable when a company wants its salespeople stationed in markets far from company headquarters or its technical problem-solvers closer to major clients.

## 2. Working Part-Time or Sharing a Job

Although downsizing your position from full-time to part-time has always been a possible option in any work environment, the idea of actually sharing a job is relatively new. Some companies now allow two people to carry out the mission of a particular position jointly (if both are qualified), although in our experience this is still a relatively rare arrangement. But each option may be available to you if you ask about it and can work out the details. You may even be able to share a job with your spouse.

## 3. Taking Advantage of Flextime

Even if your company doesn't already have an official program for you to plug into, it may be very receptive to this idea. Companies know they've got to work *with* their employees to keep them motivated and productive, so if a change in your schedule will keep you working at your best, your employer may go for it. Would coming in half an hour later and then staying half an hour later make a big difference in your life? Would starting work earlier in the day and finishing up earlier make this difference?

## 4. Becoming a Consultant or Starting a Business

This is another huge trend. More and more people are coming out of big corporations these days and declaring, "I'm never going back to that environment again!" That's fine with big business, since many large corporations now *prefer* to work with outside consultants. We've also gotten used to hearing this statement: "I've always wanted to run my own business. Maybe it's time."

What kind of business might you run? It could be directly related to your present professional skills, such as starting a consulting practice in product development, sales, engineering, or project management. Or it could be something entirely different, a real career change. We've watched people become bed-and-breakfast innkeepers, laundromat owners, acupuncturists, export/importers, international debt collectors, artists, and indexers. One of our clients even owns and operates a pushcart selling handmade greeting cards!

## 5.  Working Permanently as a Temp

Who's the biggest employer in the United States today? IBM? AT&T? General Motors? Sorry—wrong, wrong, wrong. It's a temp agency called Manpower, Inc.! Many, many professionals are now seeking greater independence in their work life, and some find that temping as a way of life is a fabulous way to achieve it. Temp agencies currently specialize in just about everything, including such formerly permanent/secure occupations as accounting, sales, and nursing. Ring up a few agencies in your local area and find out what's cookin'.

**How better to survive a job loss or shift in the fortunes of one's industry or profession than to have another income-producing line of work going at the same time?**

## 6.  Piecing Together a "Career Mosaic"

Many of our clients have chosen to build one work life from two or more careers. We're not just talking about working two or more jobs, as people have done for ages. What we mean is seriously pursuing two or more careers simultaneously, which in today's precarious work world makes terrific sense. How better to survive a job loss or shift in the fortunes of one's industry or profession than to have another income-producing line of work going at the same time? Call it insurance for the career-minded. It often makes for a more intellectually stimulating professional life overall as well.

A few of the combinations we've encountered include a history teacher/desktop publisher (profile of Alice Hale in the preceding chapter), an interior decorator/French teacher, a psychotherapist/landscaper, and a computer programmer/storyteller. What professional talents do you have wrapped up inside yourself waiting to be unveiled? Why not add one to your outside repertoire now?

## 7. Retiring!

Don't laugh! This may be more possible than you think—if not for you, then for someone you know. Have you saved enough in your IRA to let you live comfortably from here on in? Do you have a pension due that, combined with other investments, can adequately take care of your living expenses?

**Many people have the wherewithal to retire from work they no longer wish to do, and get on to something they'd enjoy, but they don't do it because of guilt or social pressure.**

Many people have the wherewithal to retire from work they no longer wish to do, and get on to something they'd enjoy, but they don't do it because of guilt or social pressure. Either they don't like the idea of people looking at them askew when they say they've retired, or they're not sure it's okay. Does it make sense, they wonder, to give up the security of a permanent job? Will family or friends feel they're no longer pulling their weight?

Once our older clients have busted through such blocks, they've gone on to do new things they've either always wanted to do or never had the chance to imagine. Former human resources professional Katherine finally left her government position to pursue a long-smoldering dream to write a book. (Gasp!) Another, Al, gave up a lucrative engineering management career after tiring of thirty years of corporate politics. He then enrolled in a lively multimedia program at Massachusetts Institute of Technology and joined his rock star son on a concert tour in Canada and Europe (as the band's roadie) . . . and lived to tell us about it!

## BALANCING ACT: OURSELVES!

Since Chloe Elizabeth arrived at our house on November 7, 1993, we've had ample opportunity to practice all of the tenets we explore in this book. Although we've always operated our business out of our home—functioning as an equal partnership, breaking through our own personal blocks, struggling to be flexible—the arrival of a little one, as all parents know, ups the ante. You can never let yourself get lazy again for very long—not in communication, not in cooking and cleaning, not even in when you get up in the morning. You've got a little living alarm clock and pacesetter to keep you in motion.

If Chloe needs to be fed, for example, or needs her diaper changed, somebody's got to get up and do it—now! If not, "someone" will hear about it. Of course, we could set very clear demarcation lines, if we wanted—Dad just does the "business work," Mom takes care of home and child. But that wouldn't fit into our combined Personal Balance Statement. "We want a happy, communicative, fun family life and a prosperous, stimulating business partnership." That fairly sums up our life goals.

A couple or business partnership may create one mutually agreed-upon Personal Balance Statement (as we did) or two individual statements that share common goals and values. Whatever the arrangement, establishing a definition of personal balance that suits you both and what you want in life is important.

### Balance Check

- How clear are you about your *personal* goals in your Personal Balance Statement?
- What sacrifices are you willing to make to achieve them?
- What ways have others chosen to achieve the same goals that wouldn't work for you?

The reality of our days often breaks down into more child care for Mom and more "job care" for Dad. But that's O.K.

Running a business out of the home still means Dad can take over parental duties more frequently than he ever could if he were away all day at an office. It means too that sometimes Mom can log a little computer time or take part in creative development with her business partner (Dad again!). You can see, then, that both of us can be involved fully in both family and business affairs every day.

But how do we juggle it all? How do we maintain even a semblance of the working partnership we had before Chloe came to live with us? Well, that's a classroom that never ends! One great solution we've found is to double up and even triple up agenda items and do them together. If we need to talk about an upcoming project or freewheel new ideas for a book, for example, we can conduct this business while walking into town as Chloe naps in her stroller. This multitask activity handles the following items: Business meeting for us, nap for Chloe, quick pick-up of home items at the store along the way, copy shop visit for the business, exercise for both parents, outside stimulation and fresh air for all three!

### Balance Check

- How could you juggle many daily tasks, business and personal, by combining them?
- What arrangements, even if not ideal, can move you closer to a life of true balance?
- How can you get more assistance and support to keep yourself moving toward your goals?

Could we get a sitter or nanny or put Chloe in preschool so that we could both spend full-time energy concentrating on business matters? Sure, that's done all the time; it's a fine solution. But it wouldn't work for us. It just isn't a part of our Personal Balance Statement!

Chloe's mom wants to be totally involved in Chloe's early years, those years before she starts school. Barbara wants Chloe to sense a solid love and trust that will fortify her self-esteem. Ken wants never to experience the regret he's heard from other men who lament they never spent any time with their children in their earliest years. "I was always at the office trying to make a living," these men recall sadly. "I'll never get the chance to see that time or to be there again. I'm sorry about that. It's gone forever."

Central to our Personal Balance Statement is a goal of high self-esteem for everyone. Chloe's feelings of security, our involvement with her and with each other, our integration of work life and family life in such a way that we can be in constant communication with each other, *real* communication—these conditions, we believe, will bring about our vision of a "happy, communicative, fun family life and a prosperous, stimulating business partnership."

We've thus arranged our days not just for work, work, work but for "work, work, fun, work, work, fun, work, fun, fun," and then more of the same. A typical day might involve returning miscellaneous business calls, developing a workshop idea, counseling a colleague, reading Chloe her slightly chewed copy of *The Three Bears,* walking to the post office (with Chloe in her stroller, of course, and us talking business), attending a business luncheon, reading Chloe *The Three Bears* a second time, editing a book chapter or article, Ken speaking at a workshop in the afternoon while Barbara feeds Chloe a delectable bowl of Gerber's Apples and Turkey, simultaneously reading Chloe *The Three Bears* yet a few more times, and then leaping on and off the Internet at the end of the day. Not your typical nine-to-five day at the factory, we know, but it gets the job done.

**You need to gauge how well you're doing at converting your visions into real-life lifestyles. Day-to-day realities then define your effectiveness.**

Job descriptions (not just ours, but yours too!) ought to derive from Personal Balance Statements. You need to gauge how well you're doing at converting your visions into real-life lifestyles. Day-to-day realities then define your effectiveness. Compare how you spend your days to what you want to get back; then evaluate how you're doing and take more action steps. At that point you'll be able to tell whether you're truly doing your "job" and you'll know how close you're coming to your ideal of true balance.

## Balance Check

• Are there any regrets along the road of life you would like to avoid?

• How would you rate yourself in terms of how well you are doing in your "job"?

• How would you define your "job" in relation to your Personal Balance Statement? What activities do you feel are most important for you to do every day?

# CHAPTER 4

## HOW FLEXIBLE IS YOUR PLAN?

Keep changing. When you're through changing, you're through.

—Bruce Barton, American advertising executive

It used to be that you could count on things. If you worked steadily, did your job well, and didn't argue with your boss, you could count on a promotion from time to time, regular pay increases, and a gold watch and farewell party when you retired.

Once upon a time we also knew that even if we fought (a lot) with our spouse or had trouble with our kids, our marriage would still more than likely hold itself together, and the kids would eventually "mature," get a job somewhere, and settle down. You did it, your parents did it, and everyone's grandparents did it too.

There were also communist countries on the other side of the globe who were our "enemies." There were three television networks (PBS didn't count). There were stores to shop in downtown, and we took our summer vacation the first two weeks of each July.

### THINGS ARE DIFFERENT TODAY, AREN'T THEY?

We seem to be getting too comfortable with contemporary "everyday life." We watch marriages breaking up at the drop of a hat, the biggest companies going out of business, adolescents getting hooked on hard drugs, and so many other "givens" of present-day life that only occasionally do we awaken to wonder when is it ever going to end?

Answer: It probably won't. In fact, to seize any kind of control these days, you've sometimes got to stop trying to control altogether! Ride the wave, and give your plan of action a long, long line of slack. Accept what comes your way, then deal with it. With these methods you'll thrive—in spite of chaos.

Because of rampant change and unpredictability, the best, most effectively laid plans today are those that can be easily changed. Ever heard the saying, "Life is what happens to you when you're making other plans"? My, my, how true in today's world.

Our plans are as good as our readiness to revise them. In all areas—work, family, personal life—with so much uncertainty swirling about, we've got to see life as a game in which the rules keep changing. Surprise is expected.

How can you win at a game like that? Here's how: By focusing on the process as much as the end result and admitting that you only think you know where you're going. Could the bus you're on in fact be taking you somewhere else? Maybe. And if so, maybe you'll do best by making the most of the ride. In the 1980s, a popular Yuppie expression went like this: "Whoever dies with the most toys wins." Now it's, "Whoever *plays* with the most toys wins."

For a model for this, look no further than Ken's brother Ed. A financial planner in Massachusetts, Ed understands that he can't control the stock market or any other funds he supervises for his clients. All he can do is keep a vigilant watch over conditions in the market, go on his hunches, and make educated recommendations to his clients about what they should do with their investments. At any given moment, Ed will shift his clients' capital (pending their approval) into another investment vehicle. But there are no guarantees. It's

**Only by incorporating goals and action plans within a fluid framework can we in any sense control our lives in today's world. It takes continuous monitoring, evaluation, guesstimating, and calculated risk.**

all guesswork, speculation, and projection—and the readiness to move and change direction at a moment's notice.

To maintain balance in the modern world, we've got to adopt Ed's work style as our paradigm. Only by incorporating goals and action plans within a fluid framework can we in any sense control our lives in today's world. It takes continuous monitoring, evaluation, guesstimating, and calculated risk.

How flexible is *your* plan? Will it get you closer to your definition of Personal Balance or keep you stuck as conditions shift? The answer to that can be found in the answer to a similar question: How flexible are *you?* Do you stick to your plans, intentions, and ideas without wavering? Do you fly off the handle or go to pieces when someone disagrees with you or makes a surprise request? If so, how do you handle unexpected twists and turns?

## FLEX DAY

Let's explore your powers of flexibility with a little exercise we call Flex Day. For the next twenty-four hours, be as flexible as you can imagine in everything you do. If you find yourself pressed to change your plans or thinking or behavior, do so—alter your agenda, switch your point of view, walk off in a different direction without a whimper. Whether it's people disagreeing with you, a project not working out as planned, or the risk of stepping out of a familiar routine, let go of your assertiveness and your ego. When at all possible, just go with the flow.

As the day goes along, record your experiences in the space below, noting how easily you shifted your thinking, plans, or behavior at each flex point, or whether you resisted or outright refused. When you've finished, resume reading this text.

# RECORD OF MY FLEX DAY

## Evaluating Your Flex Day

How did you do? Did you find that you could readily move on, modify your plans, shift your thinking? If you resisted or refused, did you do so because you felt you really had to? Or, upon reflection, did you only *think* you had to? Did you find that you could enlarge your perspective by being open to another's point of view, seeing something differently? Or did you find yourself consumed by so much internal conflict that you just couldn't bring yourself to drop your assumptions?

Learning to be flexible may come as a huge challenge to anyone socialized in a relatively unchanging world, which includes most of us. Yet when you live in waist-deep floodwaters that keep rising treacherously every day, sooner or later you've got to build a raft or learn to swim! So to help you inject more flexibility into your plans for a balanced lifestyle, let's explore ideas that have worked for us and for others:

• *"De-whelm" thyself.* When facing a major challenge, people often get overwhelmed by the details. Result: "Analysis Paralysis," stopped action, major block.

To "de-whelm" yourself, break up the big picture and take the pressure off. You don't need to do everything at once. The Chinese have an oft-repeated saying: "A journey of a thousand miles begins with a single step." Get started one step at a time, and let single step after single step move you forward.

• *Revel in imperfection.* Symptoms of perfectionism include burnout, fatigue, headaches, frustration, low self-esteem, and poor relationships. Some fun, huh?

Not many perfectionists report attaining balance and hanging onto it. They're usually working so hard striving for it that they can't actually recognize it when it appears. Let yourself fail, make mistakes, err. It's good for you!

• *Procrastinate and prosper.* Sometimes letting things lie, or turning something over in your mind—an incubation period—will benefit you more than immediate action.

In the course of writing this book, for example, the right word, metaphor, or anecdote sometimes failed to come immediately to mind. So we moved on and came back to that sticky passage later. Our brains then processed the problem subconsciously or overnight. "Sleep on it" is more than a tired cliché, you know. By giving things a little time, you allow a built-in brain process to take place and put pieces of your mental puzzle together.

## THE WALLENDA FACTOR

**Since life is not perfect, a perfectly balanced life can never be achieved. Balance in life is more like walking a tightrope: You'll sense perfection from one fleeting moment to the next, but most of the time the wire under you will try its darnedest to throw you off.**

Since life is not perfect, a perfectly balanced life can never be achieved. Balance in life is more like walking a tightrope: You'll sense perfection from one fleeting moment to the next, but most of the time the wire under you will try its darnedest to throw you off, swinging violently each instant to the left or right. You won't get much chance to rest on your laurels.

Instead of worrying about getting thrown off the rope of life, pay close attention instead to the process of moving forward. Concentrate on what you're doing, what you want to do, and what you care to accomplish. Be positive and confident in the belief that you can succeed. Don't pour energy into thinking so much about failure and imperfections. Think success!

A tragic example of someone who unfortunately forgot all this was the great tightrope walker Karl Wallenda. In the last weeks of his life he became obsessed with the idea of falling from the wire. Throughout a long, illustrious, risky career, he'd never thought this way before. Listen to this account from *Leaders* by Warren Bennis and Burt Nanus:

Shortly after Wallenda fell to his death in 1978 (traversing a 75-foot-high wire in downtown San Juan, Puerto Rico), his wife, also an aerialist, discussed that fateful San Juan walk, "perhaps his most dangerous." She recalled: "All Karl thought about for three straight months prior to it was falling. It was the first time he'd ever thought about that, and it seemed to me that he put all his energies into not falling rather than walking the tightrope." Mrs. Wallenda added that her husband even went so far as to personally supervise the installation of the tightrope, making certain that the guy wires were secure, "something he had never even thought of doing before."

From what we learned from [our] interviews of successful leaders, it became increasingly clear that when Karl Wallenda poured his energies into not falling rather than walking the tightrope, he was virtually destined to fail.

So quit worrying about not getting everything right, although you might feel that's a sure way to factor out mistakes. Commit errors, fail, mess up. Expend too much energy on not failing (or not falling) and, ironically, you may contribute to the very outcome you fear. Learning lessons from your mistakes and growing from them may be the most valuable ingredients in the mix.

### Why Failure Is Desirable: A Nearly Perfect List

- You'll learn a lot of ways *not* to do something.
- You'll look back on a failure later in life and have something to laugh about!
- You'll learn a different way to do something.
- You'll be that much closer to getting it right.
- You'll feel alive!
- You'll have something to talk about over coffee or tea.
- It'll make great material when Hollywood comes out with a movie based on your life.

## BALANCING ACT: CARL ERIKSON

The expression "bought the farm" is a positive one for Carl Erikson. Once a successful attorney and business manager,

Erikson, 53, and his wife made a monumental decision in 1992. They simply quit city life, leaving professionalism and their urban home behind, and moved to Vermont. It was a bold decision, a scary one ("I've had my moments of abject terror," Erikson laughs now), but it was a vital one. For much of his adult life, Carl Erikson had longed to work with textiles.

"I gave up fifty years of a certain standard of values," reflects Carl, the father of three grown children. "It took some soul-searching to get to where I could make this decision. But I've come to know this is right for me, not just all right." Officially waving good-bye to a business-oriented lifestyle, a path so honored and so rewarded in our society, he moved on to a way of life less supported in every way, that of the artist and craftsman.

### Balance Check

- Could you do what Carl Erikson has done? Could you chuck it all, leave behind a highly valued standing in society for a life of financial insecurity?
- Is there a passion in your life comparable to Carl's passion for working with textiles? If so, how do you exercise it? If not, what are you doing to discover it?
- How would you have advised Carl to prepare for his career/life transition? What would you need to do to make a similar move? Would your friends and family support you in such a move?

Carl began working with textiles early in his adult life, initially as a hobby, although very quickly the hobby turned to a passion that took control of all his free time. For a long while, he could see no way to turn this passion into anything like a job with which he could support his family. People surely can't make a living at this, can they? Besides, Carl often worried, should a grown man be engaging in what historically has been a feminine pursuit?

Yet, Carl's expertise with the loom, sewing machine, and needle continued to grow. Before long, he found himself churning out the most brilliant scarves, tapestries, cloths, and robes. His enthusiasm and excitement multiplied with his expertise. He began to ask two forbidden questions: Am I certain this path truly embraces my heart and soul? And would I be willing to give up my present success, built so carefully and solidly over the years, to do this?

### Balance Check

- How would you respond to Carl's second question: would I be willing to give up my present success to do this? Would you encourage him or discourage him? Would your advice be based on facts or on presumptions?
- What does your advice to Carl say about your own approach to life? Do you follow such advice yourself?

Joining one of our programs got Carl finally "talking to people who really do do this." He also began taking classes to improve his skills, and sharing his techniques and hopes for the future with other artists. He gradually learned how to become better at his craft, how to reach a public that cared to see the work, and how to begin to make at least an artist's living. It was not going to be easy, but he began to realize that it was possible. He was knocking on the door and, in amazement, watching it slowly creak open.

These days, on warm mornings or afternoons, you can find Carl Erikson sitting on the front porch of his secluded farmhouse near Brattleboro working on his textile constructions. He displays his work in New England art galleries as he looks for that first sale. Two years after he made the move, he has not found it yet. To make ends meet, he works two part-time jobs, and his wife works, too. But there are no regrets. He's done the right thing, he declares:

> I left behind those judgments from the business world where you worship income, material benefits, "success." I've no plans any longer, no interest, no wish to go back. I couldn't imagine going back, really. The remarkable thing about my life now is

that every day I'm finding out who I really am. And that I have to do this.

### Balance Check

- What aspects of Carl's new life intrigue you? Which do you want to explore more for yourself?
- Have you ever checked out the possibilities of living in another geographical area? If you'd like to live elsewhere, what blocks you from just picking up and moving there? What could you do to break through these blocks?
- What decisions have you made in your life that displayed the same degree of flexibility and courage that Carl showed in his decisions? What personal characteristics would you need to summon to show similar flexibility and courage now?

# CHAPTER 5

## WISE COMMUNICATION

In the last analysis, what we are communicates
far more eloquently than anything we say or do.
  —Stephen Covey, American business author

It's mid-afternoon and Bob Cronin takes a frantic, unexpected call at work. It's Mary, sounding desperate. "Bob, I
can't pick the kids up at school today," she says. "My biggest
client needs that report I've been working on by five. If I
don't get it to them, I could lose the account."

Up to his ears in his own report, Bob replies, "Well, I can't
help, not today, Mary, of all days. I've got a report to get
out too. It's also due at five. I've been working at it all day."

The Cronins have a huge problem. Their children will be
stepping down the school steps at three o'clock and somebody's got to be there to meet them. Mary and Bob normally take turns picking them up and driving them to their
after-school program since both parents work fairly close to
the school. But today's an impossible day for everyone.

Or is it?

Although Bob can't see how he could take a forty-five-min-
ute break from his job today, at least he has the presence of
mind to say he'll think about it. "Let me call you back," he
tells his wife. Hanging up the phone, he swivels his chair
around toward a window and pushes away from his desk.
Okay, okay, deep breath, he thinks. It would be easy to just
say, "No, no, no, I can't do it, no way." But someone has
to do it. It's not Mary's problem, it's *our* problem. Recalling
an article he read recently on shifting mental gears, he begins

letting the emotion of the moment back off so that he can reevaluate his assumptions.

Let's see, he thinks: If I reshuffle that meeting I have at 2:45 today to tomorrow afternoon, that would get me an extra hour. Leaving the office to pick up and drop off the kids would certainly break my concentration, but by how much? How serious would that really be?

Mary *had* to get her report done by five, but did he? Bob's report was due first thing in the morning. If he stayed later at work, he could make it. He began to wriggle out from his initial rigid frame of mind.

"I can do it," he said, calling Mary back, "but it means I'll be home later than usual."

"That's okay," Mary replied. "I'm sure I'll be finished by five—I've got to be! So I can pick up the kids at the end of the day and take them home."

All the books and effective communication courses insist that speaking our minds and listening, listening, listening make for clear and connected dialogues. We agree, but we caution that what's often lacking in this advice is a little thing called feelings. Often our emotional baggage or rigid personal plans muck it all up. At such moments, we may still listen but only to refute the other and defend our own case. True communication never has a chance.

Did Bob, for example, really wish to pit his children's needs against his work? Would he want to jeopardize his wife's job just to preserve his own pre-set plans for the afternoon? We know he would not. By letting the heat of the moment pass, he could look at things from a new perspective and let Mary's communication to him ("I'm desperate, Bob—it's five o'clock or else!") get through.

## THE BASICS OF GOOD COMMUNICATION

With the help of some basic tenets, your communication can flow just as readily and produce results that work for

**If you
state your
needs,
problems,
or wishes
in terms of
their rela-
tionship to
*you*, not
your lis-
tener,
you'll be
heard.
Stating
the issue
in the form
of a rhetor-
ical ques-
tion also
helps.**

everybody. The guiding paradigm is to release your tensions and push emotional defensiveness out of the way. You can clearly see the other's point of view only when you expand your capacity to respond.

Other effective techniques include:

## 1. Play the "Name, Don't Blame" Game

We could also call it "BAM": Never "blame, accuse, or malign." If you state your needs, problems, or wishes in terms of their relationship to *you*, not your listener, you'll be heard. Stating the issue in the form of a rhetorical question also helps.

*Ineffective:* "You never clean up around here, you slob. Why do you always leave everything for me to do?"

*Effective:* "Let's think of some ways to keep the house neater. I'm bothered when I see our clothes lying around."

The second response is not as threatening. Even if the speaker doesn't leave clothing lying around himself, including himself in the problem ("our clothes") takes the edge off any accusatory inferences.

## 2. Drive Away Fear

Your boss suddenly drops a ton of new work on your desk, demanding that you get going on it "right away." No amenities, no room for protest. Just get going.

Obviously, Mr. Bigboss is just a plain old jerk with no manners who ought to be strung out on a yardarm at sea or kicked overboard, right? (Many of you are now nodding in recognition.)

But could something else be going on? Maybe Mr. Bigboss is intimidated by his own boss, or maybe he's relatively new in his role of supervisor. (Was he was ever officially trained or coached in effective management skills?)

For whatever reason, rational or not, your boss could also be secretly intimidated by *you,* fearful that you might not respond quickly enough to his request, or that you might outright refuse.

Drive your boss's fears away, as St. Patrick drove away the snakes in Ireland. (Or so they say!)

*Ineffective response:* "I'm sick and tired of getting dumped on all the time around here. You can take this work and shove it! I've got better things to do with my time."

*Alternative ineffective response (muttered under your breath):* "We'll see how fast this thing gets done, all right. Mr. Bigboss picked the wrong guy to dump this crap on today."

*Effective response:* "I can get working on this right away. Of course, I'll need your advice: Shall I put this other assignment aside? Or shall I finish up what I've been doing today and get started on this new work first thing tomorrow morning? What do you think?"

What works here is to respond in a way that allays the other party's fear. You're saying, "Yes, I hear you, but, hey, don't worry, pardner, I'm on your side, we'll get through this together." In this way, you give yourself an opening to communicate your needs too. You also enlist the other person to help you with your end of the dilemma when you ask what to do about the preexisting assignment.

## 3. Never, Never, Never Give Up!

Many of us give up too soon on our point of view, taking no for an answer, and letting someone's fears or argument or emotional reaction end the discussion. Once a discussion ends, of course, all communication ends with it. We stop negotiating, and there's no further progress.

**Adopt an attitude that your mission is to keep a dialogue going, no matter what the consequences. Refuse to accept "That's it! I don't want to talk about this anymore."**

Hanging in there in a difficult conversation, especially a confrontive one, runs against the grain of countless social signals. Teachers tell us to pipe down and pay attention. Parents answer our requests for further explanation about why we have to do something with, "Because I said so, that's why." TV and movies portray characters in heated conversations who suddenly cut off communication by walking away. Either that or the scene fades to black!

Instead, take the opposite tack. Adopt an attitude that your mission is to keep a dialogue going, no matter what the consequences. Refuse to accept, "That's it! I don't want to talk about this anymore." What would happen if you kept talking anyway? Try responding, "Well, I think it's important that we keep talking about it," and then go on to make your next point.

Keep in mind too our previous advice: Let emotions go, keep reevaluating your assumptions, and never "BAM" anyone (blame, accuse, or malign). Seek to alleviate the other's fears as you keep on talking—and listening. You'll begin resolving many seemingly hopeless problems simply because you refused to let the discussion drop.

## HOWEVER, SOMETIMES GIVING UP IS GOOD!

As we said earlier, nothing is perfect. Although many of us give up on each other too quickly during attempts at communication, sometimes giving up makes sense. After all, it takes two to tangle!

Have you given it all you've got with that impossible boss? Has a once happy, healthy relationship or marriage gone sour although you really feel you've tried everything? Does a once-solid friendship feel so totally out of sync that you've nothing left in common?

If the answer is a resounding *yes!* (Ouch! You're hurting our eardrums!), then say good–bye and move on. It's a sad fact of life, but it happens to all of us. Just be really sure that you've given it your all before making the move. Try everything, then try it all again. Do your darnedest. If that doesn't work, move on and, as baseball pitcher Satchel Paige once said, "don't look back."

Remember, it's not your job to make every relationship in life work; that would be perfection. Besides, something better may be awaiting you!

## COMMUNICATION QUIZ

Circle the multiple-choice response that best represents, in your view, positive, effective communication.

---

1.  Eric is upset with his colleague Ernie, who keeps interrupting him with questions and suggestions. How should Eric tell Ernie when is a good time to talk?

    a) "Eric, I've really got to concentrate right now. Could you make some notes of your questions and we'll go over them between four and five?"

    b) "Leave me alone right now, okay?"

    c) "I don't see why you keep bringing these matters to me. Why can't you handle them yourself?"

    d) "Why don't we talk about these issues tomorrow morning? I'll have more time then."

    e) other _____

2.  Sally wants to tell her boss she feels she deserves a raise. How should she best phrase it?

    a) "I've really been working pretty hard. Haven't you noticed?"

    b) "It's been awhile since my last raise. We really need to talk about this."

    c) "I'd like to talk to you about a raise. What I've been making just isn't very fair."

d)  "I've enjoyed working here and I try to do the best job I can. I'd like to tell you about some specific reasons I think I deserve a raise. Could I ask when would be a good time for us to talk?"

e)  other _____

3.  Will wants to tell Ruth he'd like to go hiking on their next vacation, even though she prefers the ocean. Which opening would initiate the most positive communication?

a)  "I'd like to talk about our next vacation. I've been thinking perhaps we could do something different this year."

b)  "How long are we going to keep going to the beach?"

c)  "Do you think we could work something out so our vacation is a little different this year? I've been thinking about it a lot."

d)  "You know I like the mountains. Why won't you ever go along with me?"

e)  other _____

4.  George worries that his teenage son Michael is hanging out with the wrong crowd. How could he share his concerns with Michael?

a)  "Come over here and sit down. We're going to talk about these friends of yours whether you like it or not."

b)  "Are you insane? Are you on drugs?"

c)  "Michael, I've been worried about something recently. Can we talk about it?"

d)  "I don't know how to say this, but I'm concerned about some of the friends you've been spending time with recently. I'd really like to talk to you about them."

e)  other _____

5.  Chris feels that her mother never listens to her. What approach should she take to assert her point of view?

a)  "You've got to shut up once in a while and pay attention!"

b)  "There's no point talking to you—you never listen."

c) "Lately I've been feeling as if I need to be listened to more. Can we talk about that?"
d) "I'm really upset. I just don't feel you want to hear anything I have to say."
e) other _____

*Our choices:* 1) a, d 2) d 3) a, c 4) c, d 5) c

*Our explanation:* In the final analysis, we endorse responses that take accountability for the speaker's feelings and that ask for permission to begin a sensitive discussion. Putting thoughts in the form of a question also helps to cut down on threatening statements and accusations. Remember never to "BAM"—blame, accuse, or malign! Statements that attack others, show great impatience or frustration, or hinge on sarcasm will never foster true communication or create a common ground.

## TO THANK OR NOT TO THANK

**You will stand out from the crowd and create a lasting bond with many, many people if you thank them formally.**

You will stand out from the crowd and create a lasting bond with many, many people if you thank them formally. Everybody says thank you as a matter of polite conversation at the end of a transaction or meeting, but only a scant few follow that up with something more formal—a card, a letter, a gift, or a phone message. Those who do are noticed and appreciated.

Sales trainer Tom Hopkins advises sales professionals to thank people for everything imaginable—for an actual sale, for a sales lead, for introductions to new prospects . . . even to a prospect who *did not buy!* Hopkins's philosophy is simple: Everyone is a potential friend, colleague, or resource in the future, so why not give each person you meet a positive reason to remember you? A negative one or a blah one (no follow-up response at all) does nothing to foster future good relations or assistance. An opportunity is missed.

When you go out of your way to thank a person, you are truly remembered. In his book *The Pursuit of WOW!,* Tom Peters tells about a participant in one of his seminars who had routinely showed his appreciation to others throughout a long and successful career:

> The recently retired 3M exec . . . recalled his retirement party: "Several people came up to me, one or two with tears in their eyes, and thanked me for a thank-you note, sometimes one I'd written 10 or 15 years before!" People don't forget kindness (do a quick sweep of your memory bank—I bet you'll find that car mechanic who saved the family vacation or the bakery clerk who always has a warm twinkle in her eye.)
>
> My experience (and psychological literature) bears out the potency of this simple tool. Positive reinforcement goes a long way, and most people don't give (or get) much of it.

Good communication thrives on foundations of trust and goodwill. People will go to the wall for each other when they feel appreciated. Build and keep such trust with formal thank-you's that are above and beyond the call of routine propriety.

And when you write a thank-you note, should it be in the form of a letter or a simple handwritten card? Ah, a debate as old as the ages! Unless you need to formally reiterate the high points of a business proposal or job interview, we're partial to the card approach. Handwritten notes convey a sense of interpersonal intimacy that suggests something special has occurred. They also tug at the sleeve of the person you're thanking, shouting, "Open me first!" Whenever *we* receive a handwritten card in our stack of business or junk mail, especially an unexpected one, it's the very first thing we open! We bet it's that way with you too.

## FEEDBACK THAT WORKS!

Communication is an ongoing process that functions best when two or more people feel comfortable letting their ideas and feelings flow. When such ideas and feelings include feedback about how a relationship is going or how work is progressing, the communication contributes to a lasting, fulfilling, productive partnership or team over time.

Engage the following rules about feedback and you'll rarely go wrong.

## When You Need to Give Negative Feedback, Always Give Positive Feedback in the Same Breath

It's the old "I've got good news and I've got bad news" device. Start with the good news (positive feedback). Find something to applaud or compliment. It's not just a case of being flattering. We're talking here about remembering to stay positive and to keep track of what someone is doing right. In a rush to correct a problem, people often forget about the effective aspects of something, thus throwing the baby out with the bathwater!

**EXAMPLE:** "Jim, let's talk about how our project is going. You've been successful in getting everyone's attention with your product presentation—prospects are really coming out of the wall and we should be able to do some terrific business. I feel really good about that.

"Now let's talk a little about finalizing sales. Our numbers haven't been as good as we'd like, and I thought perhaps a skill-building workshop in closing a sale might improve your ratio. Do you think that such a workshop would be helpful to you? I'd like to hear your ideas on what we could do together."

**Give *helpful feedback by:***

- Voicing your feelings. ("I feel really good about that.")
- Describing implications of what you see happening. ("We should be able to do some terrific business.")
- Avoiding being judgmental or using labels.

- Posing statements and "inclusive" questions. ("Do you think that a workshop would be helpful to you? I'd like to hear your ideas on what we could do together.")

Get *helpful feedback by:*

- Appreciating and acknowledging feedback you receive.
- Exploring what you're hearing by asking questions.

**EXAMPLE:** Jim might respond to his supervisor by saying, "I appreciate what you're telling me. I've felt good about my presentations, and I'm glad they've been having an effect in raising product attention. What sales ratio are we shooting for that we're not meeting? What skills do you think I need to improve? Can you tell me more about this workshop you'd like me to attend?"

## Sensitive Areas

We all need to face difficult discussions covering sensitive areas in our relationships. If you remember never to "BAM" (blame, accuse, or malign), you'll keep many potential confrontations from blowing up in your face.

**If you remember never to "BAM" (blame, accuse, or malign), you'll keep many potential confrontations from blowing up in your face.**

A useful "script," recommended by many communications experts, involves stating your case without judgment, expressing your feelings, and then giving specific reasons for your feelings. After pausing to hear the other person's comments, you describe the change you would like, give your reasons for wanting such a change, and then invite the other to respond. Here's an example:

*Mary:* Bob, when you make arrangements for a big purchase like that new CD system for our car, I get nervous because I'm afraid we can't afford it. We've been trying to add to the kids' college funds as much as we can, and I haven't let myself even think about luxuries for either of us.

*Bob:* I didn't think it would be a problem. I have those long drives to the branch offices every week and I guess I wanted a little something to make them more tolerable.

*Mary:* I understand that. I don't want to restrict either of us more than necessary. What I'd like is for you to consider talking with me about big purchases beforehand, and I'll be willing to do the same with you. Maybe there's a way for us to put our heads together and get *some* of the things we'd like but never allow ourselves.

*Bob:* I guess I can do that. Hey, maybe we could make a list now of some luxuries both of us would like, then plan out a budget over the next year. I'll bet we could eventually knock a few items off our list without seriously cutting into the kids' college funds.

That's an effective approach. No attacks, no blame, just a spirit of "Let's work it out."

But can you imagine how this conversation would have gone if Mary had begun: "Hey, Bob, who gave you the right to go off on your own and throw money away on a fancy CD system for yourself? Did we just win Publisher's Clearinghouse and I didn't hear about it? Forget about college for our children—Big Bob has to play his little music box in the car."

That opening would've gotten Bob's attention, right? But then what?

## QUOTATIONS FROM CHAIRMAN COVEY

Stephen Covey's work offers numerous insights and much wisdom when it comes to personal growth and balance. In particular, his two best-selling business books, *Seven Habits of Highly Effective People* and *Principle-Centered Leadership*, are gold mines of ideas for improving communication and resolving conflict. Here's a sampling of our favorites:

Communication is primarily a function of trust, not of technique. When the trust is high, communication is easy, it's effortless, it's instantaneous, and it's effective—it works. But when the trust is low and the Emotional Bank Account is overdrawn, communication is exhausting, it's terribly time-consuming, and it's like walking around a minefield.

"Seek first to understand" involves a very deep shift in paradigm. We typically seek first to be understood. Most people do not listen with the intent to understand; they listen with the intent to reply. They're either speaking or preparing to speak. They're filtering everything through their own paradigms, reading their autobiography into other people's lives.

If they have a problem with someone—a son, a daughter, a spouse, an employee—their attitude is, "That person just doesn't understand."

In empathic listening, you listen with your eyes and with your heart. You listen for feeling, for meaning. You listen for behavior. You use your right brain as well as your left. You sense, you intuit, you feel. Empathic listening is powerful because it gives you accurate data to work with.

# CHAPTER 6

## TIME AS AN ALLY

*Time is the coin of your life. It is the only coin you have, and only you can determine how it will be spent.*

—Carl Sandburg, American writer

It's not the time exactly, it's our anxiety about time that really gets to us. We set deadlines (or deadlines are set for us), and then we rush, rush, rush to meet them. We spend inordinate amounts of energy fretting over the often very real possibility that we may in fact *not* meet our deadlines. This happens despite an understanding that deadlines can never be more than guidelines, imprecise attempts to predict how long something will take, predictions against which we then match our efforts.

The drum-drum drumbeat of deadlines often fills us with a sense of finality that doesn't really need to be. In fact, so many of our attitudes about time are shaped by images of dread: time crunch, time's running out, no time left. Yet one of two compensating principles is often at work:

1. *"Work expands to fill the time."* When deadlines are overly generous or pessimistic about how long something will take, giving us *more* time than we need, we tend to use up all the extra time, filling it in, stretching out the work.

2. *"Coming through in the clutch."* When time is considered short, we tend to make an extra commitment to meet a deadline, taking shortcuts, working longer hours, delegating or subcontracting parts of the work. We do what we can to work faster.

Thus, the good news about time is that you can control it as well as be controlled by it. This all depends on your frame of mind. Time, after all, is a mental construct. We the people invented clocks, watches, and sundials—they didn't exist before we came along. So how you choose to perceive time—that you've got plenty of it or never enough—dictates your power in relation to it.

## TEST YOUR ATTITUDES TOWARD TIME

Does time control you, or do you control time? Consider the following statements about time. Which comes closest to your attitudes and your lifestyle?

1. There's never enough time. From the start of the day until I hit the sack at night, I'm always just running, running, running, playing catch-up. And I never make it.
2. I'm always doing so many things at once. While eating lunch, I review reports and make and take phone calls. At home, I'm reading the paper, making dinner, and playing with the kids at the same time. I even go through my to-do list in my head during my aerobics class. I just wish there were another way to get everything done.
3. I wish I could get some time just for me. But I'm always getting calls at work from family or friends about some emergency. Even in my car, they call me—I'm like an ambulance chaser! I just can't seem to get away.
4. I'm always late. No matter how hard I try, I can't get out of the house early enough. I always notice three or four little things I figure I can get out of the way before I leave. They always take longer than I thought they would.
5. I have a lot of time on my hands I don't know what to do with. I'm not employed at the moment, and there are only so many want ads you can look at, so

many resumés you can mail. After that, what's there to do all day? I get really bored.

Can you see how these time problems are in fact created by each person? It's really attitudes about time we're talking about, isn't it? People's anxieties derive from their mental decisions about what must be done and what can't be avoided. Time itself has nothing to do with it!

Now let's explore a few ideas for resolving these particular time problems. For each of the preceding statements, what suggestions could you make to the person? See the accompanying worksheet.

## ADVICE FOR THE TIME-TRAPPED

If you were writing a column called "Time Advisor," how would you counsel readers who wrote to you about the time management problems described on page 60?

1. Dear "Playing Catch-Up,"

_____

_____

_____

_____

_____

2. Dear "Everything at Once,"

_____

_____

_____

_____

_____

3. Dear "Ambulance Chaser,"

_____

_____

_____

_____

_____

4. Dear "Always Late,"

_____

_____

_____

_____

_____

5. Dear "Really Bored,"

_____

_____

_____

_____

_____

## TIME PROBLEMS

Now take a look at your own time problems. What's your perception of time and your relationship to it? List below your most prevalent time issues. Some may correspond to the examples above; others might be unique to you.

# MY PERSONAL TIME PROBLEMS

Fill out the space below with as many of your personal time problems as you can think of.

We'll now list solutions to common time problems recommended by time experts and by people who have resolved their own issues. As you read through this list, note any you might adopt for yourself.

1. *Steer clear of "meeting junkies."* To the extent possible, call and attend meetings only when necessary. Do most business one-to-one or by memo. Stay away from people who can't wait to herd you (and everybody else) into the conference room. (There are more meeting-reduction ideas later in this chapter.)

2. *Double up on activities.* Read work materials when on trains or planes. Bunch up errands and appointments to cut down on travel and transition time. Dance, listen to music, or sing your favorite tunes as you work around the house.

3. *Delegate!* You don't have to do everything yourself, you know.

4. *Keep your desk and office in order.* Throw away old paperwork and reading materials. File things so that they're easy to find.

5. *Use daily and weekly to-do lists.* Keep magic markers around for circling priorities (first, second, third, etc.) in colors. Make nagging activities first priority. Also do the hardest and most time-sensitive tasks first. Keep in mind the catchphrase of a jazz drummer we know: "D. I. N.," he says, emphatically. Translation: "Do It Now!" He's never been late for a gig yet!

6. *Grant yourself some privacy.* Whether at home or at work, take time to concentrate or reflect on things. Shut off your phone, put a "Do Not Disturb" sign on your door, shut off TV or radio.

7. *Keep a time log.* Periodically evaluate how effectively you're using your time. Write everything down and the time it takes, and then review it.

8. *Set deadlines for yourself and others.* People use their time more productively when they put tasks within a time frame. Plan when you want to finish. (But be flexible! Remember, a deadline is only a guideline.)

**If you remember that your relationship with time has everything to do with preconceived notions, you can begin successfully employing time as a guideline to keep you moving through the task at hand.**

Now go back to your personal list of time problems. Which ideas will solve which of your problems? Write a solution or idea beside each problem.

If you remember that your relationship with time has everything to do with preconceived notions, you can begin successfully employing time as a guideline to keep you moving through the task at hand. When you need more time, ask for it, or give yourself permission to expand your deadline and move things in your schedule around. When you have too much time on your hands, fill it with useful, satisfying, fun, stimulating activities. You can always have enough time if you want it, and you can always find ways to use it to your best advantage.

## THE LIMITLESS EAR

Everyone's had friends who call up on the phone and don't want to get off. Barbara had such a friend once upon a time who loved to analyze every detail of every date with every new boyfriend, no matter what took place. There was always great melodrama in her tales, including pathos, ecstasy, agony, and confusion. Needless to say, it was tough at times for Barbara to simply get the hell off the phone!

One day this friend paid Barbara a compliment, or so she thought, referring to her as The Limitless Ear. "Barbette, you'll always listen to everything I've got to say, won't you?" But Barbara didn't really *want* to listen, exactly. Like many of us, she just never knew how to cut her friend, The Limitless Mouth, off.

Rather than waste hours, days, years on the phone, we've come up with what we call "close-out" suggestions. Because of these we never have to stay on the phone longer than we want to. Here are a few ways to get off:

- Say quickly, "Hey, I gotta run." Our favorite. Seems too simple to be true, but believe us, it's very effective.

- End the conversation by chiming, "I've got another call coming in."
- Don't ever return a Limitless Mouth's phone calls. Just ignore, forget about, delay returning such calls. Note: This remedy will need to be employed a few times before it works. Limitless Mouths have incredible staying power.
- Cut yourself off in the middle of your own sentence. The other party will think you were both cut off and will try to call you back right away, so don't answer your phone for a while. In fact, keep it off the hook for a few hours—or days!
- Screen messages with your answering machine. Pick up only when you really want to.
- Tell the truth: *"I want to get off the phone now!"*

### Balance Check

- Do you sometimes let time get the best of you? You can always manage your time if you don't let your time manage you. Get your internal priorities in sync, and you'll activate an internal time-sensitive alarm system that will dispense time in allotments that support your desires. You *can* take a phone call while you're in the middle of a heavy concentrated activity, for example, or you can make one. But *you* must control how long the call will last.
- Do you know how to practice intuitive time management? Your number one priority is to act on what is nagging at you on your to-do list. Never mind what you think you should do first or what seems logical. What's hanging back there in your mind, eating away at you, bugging you? What is it you just can't forget about? Whatever it is, go out and get it done. Then move on to what nags at you next.

## SLOWING DOWN TIME

Since time is a function of your perception, you naturally have dominion over its pace. Time will go very fast when you're in a state of flow, that is, at one with the activity you're engaged in. Likewise, time bogs down to a snail's crawl when you're out of sync with your behavior. Be lucky enough to attend a terrific, suspenseful, well-acted, superbly directed movie and time will fly by like (snap!) that! Try sitting through a dog, however, and, well . . . Zzzzzz. You know what we mean.

Anything boring slows time down. So, too, anything you have to wait for. But you can change all that by getting interested in something while you're waiting or bored. Should you find yourself in a slow-moving check-out line at the supermarket, for example, pick up a magazine while you're standing there—Hey, that's why they put them there, right? If you sink into a snappy article about your favorite movie star or supermodel, your check-out line will accelerate to warp speed!

We know another way to slow time down, though, this one without getting bored. In fact, this method is something of a paradox because normally time goes faster when you're really interested in something. Again, it's your perception of time that's at work, not time itself.

Pick up a small object, like an orange or a pencil, and begin examining it closely. Look carefully at all its features, telling yourself you've got all the time in the world. Marvel at the way it's made, check out its surface features, examine any indentations you can see, the shape, the color—everything. "Take" your time, so to speak. Slowly, thoroughly, examine the entire object.

Before long, you'll begin feeling your body rhythm slowing down. You won't care about time or clocks; you won't feel as though time has much velocity at all. You'll also feel something warm in your gut: calm, peace, security—dare we say it?—a sensation of balance! Yet you probably won't have spent much "real" time doing this exercise at all.

When you're frazzled, fried, at odds, confused, scared, upset, rushed, or in any other state of being that keeps you from feeling in control or safe or sane, try this technique. Although you may not have literally learned to slow time down, you'll feel as though you have. And you may also feel as though you created a sense of balance. Yes, that easily, and immediately. Instant balance!

## FEWER MEETINGS EQUALS MORE TIME!

It's all too easy to call a meeting or to show up for one and assume that you're engaging in productive work. Yet time management experts continually insist that professionals attend far too many meetings and, worse, that most meetings are frequently unnecessary, too long, and wander far afield from their original agendas.

Can you refuse to go to many of the meetings you currently attend? Can you call fewer meetings yourself? Can you make meetings shorter, more to the point, worth going to?

Here are a few suggestions for keeping meetings from getting in the way of your real work:

**Can you refuse to go to many of the meetings you currently attend? Can you call fewer meetings yourself? Can you make meetings shorter, more to the point, worth going to?**

• *Call meetings at the end of the day, particularly Friday.* People will want to get done with the meeting faster and will be less inclined to stray from relevant matters and talk on and on and on about every aspect of a problem or its possible solutions.

• *Have everyone stand at meetings.* People don't want to stand for long if they don't have to, so once again you'll observe participants getting on with the business at hand and being less inclined to drag it out. Keep chairs out of the room, if at all possible.

• *Attend sections of meetings, not whole meetings.* Some meetings may directly involve you only in certain topics or in pieces of larger business matters. If you can predict which point in a meeting will matter to you personally, just plan on being there for that portion of the meeting only.

• *Schedule meetings and appointments back to back.* We use

this technique all the time, and it works marvelously! By scheduling a meeting up against the current one, you pressure yourself to get down to substantive business at once. You quickly learn to handle matters economically and, like everything else in life, you get better and better at it the more you do it. No matter how your meeting goes, it definitely will end at an appointed time.

- *Settle business at once.* Often someone wants to sit down with you for a meeting on a matter that can be settled on the spot. When someone requests a meeting with you for any reason, ask what he or she wants to talk about. Then try talking it out right away. You can often resolve things in a five- or ten-minute talk, eliminating that hour or two a meeting might have lasted.

## HOW MUCH DO YOU NEED TO KNOW?

**You frequently don't really need to talk out a problem for as long as you think you do before getting down to the principal business of being a practical problem solver.**

Tests of human creative problem-solving abilities have shown that people often need much less time to study a subject or problem than they think. In one test, two groups were given the same problem to analyze but under very different set-up conditions. Members of the first group could take all the time they felt they needed to ask questions about the problem at hand, analyzing the problem to death if they wanted to. Those in the second group were allowed only two minutes to ask questions about the problem and then begin freewheeling as many solutions as they could come up with.

The first group's analysis went on for forty-five minutes, yet the two-minute group far outshone the first in terms of both quality and quantity of creative solutions proposed.

Conclusion? You frequently don't really need to talk out a problem for as long as you think you do before getting down to the principal business of being a practical problem solver. So avoid meetings like the plague!

# FITNESS TIME TIPS

Arnold Schwarzenegger wants you to know that you can stay fit no matter how hectic your work schedule or home life. To illustrate, he tells a story about a day he checked into his hotel with only thirty minutes to spare before he had to get ready for an important meeting. He had not done his workout that day and wouldn't be able to later, given his busy schedule.

Slapping on a pair of athletic shoes and donning his sweat-suit, he headed for the hotel staircase. Within ten minutes he had bounded up to the roof of the hotel, twenty floors in all. Once at the top, he turned around and bounded back! In twenty minutes he had covered forty floors, twenty flights up and twenty down. Thus concluded Arnold's personal aerobics class for the day!

How can you emulate The Terminator's impromptu solution? Can you make certain your fitness plans don't go the way of the family farm and stimulating evening conversation? Scan the following list of suggestions for piggybacking your fitness activities onto your home and business duties. Remember, blocks we refuse to let go are called excuses.

- Park your car at the far end of the parking lot at work or the shopping mall and walk the rest of the way.
- Take your kids to a park and play ball with them.
- Hop onto your NordicTrack or rowing machine while watching the evening news on TV.
- Bike to work or your friend's house or to do errands.
- Choose a colleague or business partner as your work-out buddy so that you can talk business as you ride the Lifecycle or spot each other at the weightlifting bench.

# CHAPTER 7

## FOLLOW THE
## LEADER—YOURSELF!

Everyone is in the best seat.

—John Cage, American composer

Hundreds of ideas, sparks, lightning bolts zip through our heads every day, indeed every second! Somehow we pick out one and think more deeply about it, say it out loud, or do something about it. Our choices define how we spend our time, our energy, our lives.

When we choose to revel in negativity, for example, or feel victimized or incapable of something, we have no one to "BAM" (blame, accuse, or malign) but ourselves. However, when we choose to embark on a positive path—that we're strong, able, confident, determined, up to a challenge—we then direct all our efforts to bringing this option to reality. As Captain Picard of the Starship *Enterprise* might say, we've chosen to "make it so." Each such choice sets the stage for our behavior and maps out potential results.

Suppose your boss asks you to work late one night although you've made other plans. You've been looking forward to stepping out on this night for a long time—you've got tickets to a hit play—but suddenly there he is, big stack of paperwork in both arms, heading your way. "This has got to be done tonight," Mr. Bigboss tells you. "They've been waiting for it in marketing all week." You begin muttering as Mr. Bigboss strolls away. "Why, that no-good, son of a . . . Why tonight of all nights? Why me? Arrrghhh!"

You grumble, you feel angst, you feel horrible. The whole world's against you. But why do you react this way?

Some people will say it's only natural, that they can't help but feel this way; it's the way we're all built. That's not true, of course—we really can learn to react any way we like. Although it might mean training ourselves to think and react differently, or to incorporate new perspectives into our world view, or undergoing intensive inner examination of how we've come to believe what we believe, time and again individuals who've made an inner commitment to adopt new ways of acting and reacting have successfully made the switch.

Participants in our career programs, for example, frequently express great anxiety over the prospect of making phone calls to people they don't know. "What will I say to them? What will they say to me?" they ask.

"Honesty is the best strategy," we reply. "Just tell them what's on your mind—that you're exploring a career change and you want to learn more about the work they do." A typical reaction to us is: "But why would they talk to me? What if they hang up on me? What if I get yelled at for bothering them?"

One week later, our anxious career explorers strut in with a fresh perspective, relating glowing tales of friendly, generous, stimulating new friends. One contact wouldn't stop talking; another invited our client to lunch. These experiences alter our clients' attitudes in relation to the phone and to approaching strangers with their career questions. They begin looking forward to the positive rewards of career calls to people they don't know. Anxiety levels drop precipitously.

Every experience, even so-called negative ones, can be positive and lead to insight. Everything that happens to you can help you grow. It's self-limiting attitudes that blind many people to this. They choose to see something as good or bad, dark or light, positive or negative. Their perspective reflects their current level of balance.

How about your theater tickets, for example? Could such a "revoltin' development," as Chester A. Riley (William Bendix) used to say on TV, be classified in any way as a positive, learning experience? You cancel a terrific evening, blow off eighty-five dollars on the tickets alone, and—indignity of indignities—spend most of the night at your desk! How could this be good?

In the space below, we invite you to freewheel positive ways to view this situation. How many can you think of?

## HOW WORKING LATE CAN BE GOOD!

Fill up this space with as many ideas as you can think of.

How'd you do? Was this a difficult exercise or a breeze? By pondering this scenario, did you come up with a few positive gains that your initial reactions might not have allowed for? Now take a look at the list that we came up with. These are not definitive answers, just our own ideas.

---

> **HOW WORKING LATE CAN BE GOOD!**
>
> - It gives me a chance to practice the art of thinking positively.
> - It gives me the chance to complete my business project successfully and feel good about my work.
> - I can give my theater tickets away and make someone else happy.
> - I can demonstrate to myself how unattached I am to "things."
> - It gives my boss the chance to recognize how dedicated I am to my work.

---

**Once you learn to react positively to events and interactions of your life, you can graduate to *creating* positive events and interactions. That's when you start routinely setting events in motion—inspiring, initiating, and actually shaping your reality.**

By genuinely rethinking your emotional reactions to things and then reframing situations in a positive light, you can turn the darkest of experiences into bright days of sunshine. Practice this again and again and you'll begin reacting more positively to events as they happen.

## SHAPING REALITY

Once you learn to react positively to events and interactions of your life, you can graduate to *creating* positive events and interactions. That's when you start routinely setting events in motion—inspiring, initiating, and actually shaping your reality. That's when you become a leader of all that's around you, a master of your domain.

Do we mean by this forcing yourself on others, making people do your bidding by intimidation or manipulation? Uh-uh, no, nein, pas du tout. Force and power plays may gain in the short run but not much longer than that. People will go along with you to get along, but the first chance they see, they'll strike back with a vengeance. That's why dictators so often go down in flames.

## QUALITIES I'VE ADMIRED IN A MENTOR

Can you recall a teacher or boss who inspired you, someone you truly admired, for whom you would have done anything, from whom you learned something valuable? In the space below, list five qualities you can think of that best describe this person:

1. _____

2. _____

3. _____

4. _____

5. _____

What did you come up with? Probably what you wrote is mostly positive. There may be a negative or two as well (after all, nobody's perfect!), but in general those who inspire us and help us grow also treat us with respect and give us room to make our own decisions. They do not try to control us, and they never treat themselves or others badly.

## APPRECIATION LIST

Make a list of people you appreciate for the balance they bring to their lives. Under each name, explain why you specifically chose that person for this list. What guidelines can you adopt or strive for to help you achieve balance in your own life?

1. NAME: _____

   Why chosen: _____

   _____

2. NAME: _____

   Why chosen: _____

   _____

3. NAME: _____

   Why chosen: _____

   _____

4. NAME: _____

   Why chosen: _____

   _____

5. NAME: _____

   Why chosen: _____

   _____

6. NAME: _____

   Why chosen: _____

   _____

# JOINING YOUR APPRECIATION LIST

What skills, characteristics, and behaviors can you adopt, based on those people you placed on your Appreciation List? Your goal is to put yourself in the same company as those you appreciate:

1. _____

2. _____

3. _____

4. _____

5. _____

**The discomfort of fear is a sign of growth in progress. By leaving behind your comfort zone and journeying into unfamiliar, alien territory, you embark on adventure, intrigue, and new knowledge.**

## EMBRACING FEAR

Often people use fear as an excuse to run away from something. "I'm not comfortable with that," they say, whether it's committing to marriage, asking for a raise, enrolling in graduate school, or apologizing for some transgression.

But the discomfort of fear is a sign of growth in progress. By leaving behind your comfort zone and journeying into unfamiliar, alien territory, you embark on adventure, intrigue, and new knowledge. You achieve things, you affect others' lives, you move mountains.

How comfortable were the civil rights activists of the 1950s and 1960s? How comfortable was Sir Edmund Hillary as he froze his way up Mount Everest? How comfortable is giving birth? How comfortable is learning to drive a car, studying trigonometry, or struggling through a foreign language? Obviously each experience teaches people something they're proud of forever; while they're doing it they know that the end result will be worth all the discomfort.

Go back now to your Personal Balance Statement and your Agenda of Desire. Consider specific steps you need to take to achieve your definition of Personal Balance. What fears does each step provoke? What positive lessons or outcomes do you foresee as you meet each challenge?

| Step | Fear | Lesson |
|------|------|--------|
| 1. _____ | _____ | _____ |
| 2. _____ | _____ | _____ |
| 3. _____ | _____ | _____ |
| 4. _____ | _____ | _____ |
| 5. _____ | _____ | _____ |
| 6. _____ | _____ | _____ |

# DON'T LET GUILT DRAW YOU DOWN

In most cases, guilt implies that you've done something wrong or could have done a thing differently when in fact you usually do the best you can with the facts before you and your level of experience and knowledge. Guilt draws you down and keeps you down. It prevents you from growing and learning from your experiences. Although guilt may be a useful emotion when we *have* done something wrong (committed a heinous crime, for example), most of the time it simply holds us back.

For example, suppose you forgot to send a birthday card to your mother because you were busy all week with work and the kids. You could choose to feel terribly guilt-ridden for being such a "bad" daughter or son, or you could shrug it off and immediately send a belated card or present, or you could make a call and say, "Mom, I'll make it up to you. Dinner on Thursday night? On me, of course!" In other words, don't get anxious about it—*do* something about it!

On a more serious level, what if you blew a really big account at work? The company's client felt your work wasn't up to snuff, for one reason or another, so your boss takes you off the account. You've got two choices here: 1) You can feel down, down, down, reach for a drink (or two or three), mope around, and tell yourself that you're an incompetent, unworthy wretch. Or 2) you could find out what went wrong! You can go right to your boss and say with confidence, "Can we talk about what happened? I've got to learn from this, so I can improve and grow."

You adopt the attitude that life after all is a learning experience and that sometimes we fail and sometimes we win; that's just the way it goes. Wasting long hours regretting the past only drains us of what could be energized, productive, stimulating hours in the present and future. Thus, guilt is an indulgence that anyone seeking balance cannot afford. So step up to a mirror today and declare yourself, "Not guilty!"

# BALANCING ACT: BOB RICHARD

When Bob Richard got laid off after twelve years as a test developer with a government personnel division, the incident turned him into a self-described basket case. At 43, he wondered where else he might work, what else he might do. He was utterly shaken.

Sensing the need for a support structure to get him through what he foresaw as a potentially painful transition, he decided to join a job-search support group. Such an action was a major one for Bob because he'd always studiously avoided groups of any kind. He'd always been scared of them.

"I'd just never been comfortable in a group," he said. "I never enjoyed the atmosphere of groups, or the dynamics, or the participation required. People always seemed to take to groups more naturally than I ever did. It made me tremendously self-conscious. I can't explain why I felt this way, but I always had, all my life, and I'd never been able to shake it."

This time, Bob was willing to risk all because he could imagine the benefits. The danger from trying to wing his way through a period of unemployment, at a time when there was so much competition around, seemed a vastly greater risk.

### Balance Check

- Can you empathize with Bob's anxiety? Is there something in your life that everyone else seems to handle easily but you try to avoid? Have you ever talked to anyone about this issue to see whether you're truly that alone in your feelings about it?
- What risk would you be willing to take to get yourself through a crisis despite your fears? Would you be willing to actually initiate something you fear, as Bob did—go directly into it in order to conquer it?

As Bob began looking around for a group to join, he encountered a huge block almost immediately: He couldn't find one! Any group he located met too far from his home or met too infrequently. He realized one day with a major shudder that if he wanted to join a job-search group at this point in his life, he'd have to stand up and start one himself!

Initially he figured he'd offer his living room one night a week to a handful of unemployed professionals. He'd sit quietly in the back and just serve the coffee.

> But the first night I was startled to find that, far from feeling anxious in my little group, I found myself enjoying it! It was amazing, thrilling! It was one of those rare moments when suddenly you learn something very new about yourself that you never knew before. I could enjoy taking part in a group. I was hooked.

He really was. Before long, Bob Richard found himself not only coordinating his own "little" group (which grew steadily until he had to move it out of his living room into a church hall) but also assisting other fledgling job-search group leaders as they struggled to get their own groups started. Though he endured the usual "learning curve"— the normal mistakes and stumbles along the way that teach us new skills—eventually he graduated to running bigger and bigger groups and even founding and administering a statewide coalition of job-search group facilitators.

As a result of all this experience, Bob was offered a position as a workshop leader and group facilitator with a quasi-governmental agency. Ultimately he became known to training professionals all across the state as "The Group Guy." Bob Richard had become a "groupie" in a big way. As he explains it:

> I've come to love the process of helping individuals learn from each other through a group format. When leading workshops in my current job, I find I can relate to people's feelings very well because I've often been through a similar struggle in my

own life. I've had people break down crying in one of my groups over a personal problem, and I can instantly develop a rapport with them and foster the right group support. That helps them through it.

This kind of experience has added a new dimension to my life that's made me feel worthwhile. It affects my personal life too. When I'm preparing a workshop, my wife sees me walking around the house smiling to myself. That makes for a happier home life for everybody. I'm lucky to have found this.

### Balance Check

- What moments similar to Bob's experiences can you recall in your lifetime? When have you suddenly learned something about yourself that you never knew before?
- What people skills do you possess that can help others through a struggle? How can you employ these skills in your work and home life in ways that might generate more balance not only for you but also for those around you?
- Do you have any special interests or passions, à la Bob's love of groups, that you could use to improve your professional life? Can you see how just doing what came naturally, that is, his volunteer activities with groups, led Bob to a fulfilling balance in both his work and his personal life?

# CHAPTER 8

## THE HUMAN TOUCH

Angels fly because they take themselves lightly.

—G. K. Chesterton, British writer

They were tired, there was no getting around that. Mary, Bob, and the kids had just spent a long day driving through three states on the first day of their vacation. They were now headed for a country inn.

"Only five more miles," Mary said, looking at the map. "Turn down this country road." The scenery all around them was postcard-perfect, with mountains in the distance and a gushing river by the side of the road. Everyone looked forward to getting out of the car in the next few minutes and sitting down to a sumptuous country meal.

Then the unthinkable happened. The car began to rattle and shake. Bob and Mary looked at each other. "What *is* that?" Bob asked the heavens. More rattling, louder this time. Trouble. Their kids in the back seat abandoned their Power Rangers momentarily and listened carefully.

The car began to lurch. Oh, this is rich, Bob thought, his stomach sinking. "What's wronggg?" Mary groaned. All at once, the car gasped, lurched a last, terrible time, and died in the middle of the road.

Bob hurried out to look under the hood. After a few minutes, Mary joined him. Neither knew much about cars but both knew one thing—a few short miles from their destination, with night creeping in all around them, they weren't going anywhere.

The kids started whining in the back seat. "I'm hungry," Jeannie cried. "Let's go, go," wailed Bob, Jr. "Bafroom," Sarah said quietly.

It was the worst of times, it was the worst of times. No cars came by. The sun went down behind the mountains. "I'll have to walk to the inn for help," said Bob. It seemed the only solution.

"Be careful," Mary called after him. The kids didn't know what to say as they watched their father trudge down the road. Except for Sarah. "Bafroom," she repeated, more loudly this time.

I can't believe this is happening, Mary sighed. Everything looked pretty bleak. Until all of a sudden Bob made a reverse turn in the road, began twirling himself around, flapping his arms and honking like a goose! "Onk, onk, onk!" he bellowed, weaving from side to side on the empty road, skipping into the air, as if trying to fly.

**Studies of those who live into their nineties or a second century consistently show that high among the most common characteristics of elders is a healthy sense of humor.**

Mary wondered what was going on. Then, as the kids began to laugh, she realized. "Daddy's funny," Jeannie giggled. "Daddy is a bird," cried Bob, Jr., flapping his arms too. "Yes, Daddy's a funny bird," Mary agreed, tears in her eyes from laughing. Sarah no longer needed a bafroom.

Studies of those who live into their nineties or a second century consistently show that high among the most common characteristics of elders is a healthy sense of humor. Studies of good marriages reveal the same—those who stay together for the longest periods, couples reporting high levels of satisfaction with each other and the best communication, share a common sense of humor. In the workplace, too, if you're sociable and friendly, if you can let go the heaviness of tough situations, you'll add immense value to your presence, not to mention your own inner stability.

Since balance is more accurately measured internally than externally, the contributions of humor cannot be denied. Do you laugh enough in your day, whether at home or work? Would you like to laugh more? Do you make others laugh? If difficult situations are opportunities to learn, what happens when you take this idea one step further and see difficulties as an opportunity to laugh?

Of all the professional advice for alleviating stress, generating true communication, working well with others, and generally feeling good, none is more naturally understood or easily accessed than humor and fun. When everything's gone wrong, when calamity strikes, when your life feels like it's going down the tubes, laughter can always bring you back. It can restore that sense of wholeness and steadiness also known as balance.

As with other aspects of balance covered in this book, this one's up to you. When a thought strikes you to get wacky sometime, why not go with it? Bob broke everyone's tension just by waving his arms up and down and honking like a bird. No great skills demanded, no preparation, no tools, just a simple, spontaneous outburst caused by a nutty idea. Yet how it transformed everyone's mood and perception of the experience! Everyone came out a winner.

## FOURTEEN WACKY WAYS TO ACHIEVE MORE BALANCE IN YOUR LIFE

Let yourself go nuts here! What are fourteen crazy ideas that could bring more balance into your life? You may never do any of these things, but you can have fun thinking about them! Sketch them out or list them in the space below.

**Your will-
ingness to
be human,
to touch
others in
your life,
to be open
to new ex-
periences,
to listen to
and
respond to
others, to
learn from
everything
and every-
one, to
make
those
around you
laugh—all
these qual-
ities are
keys to
balance.**

## A WILLINGNESS TO BE HUMAN

Inside all of us lie a generosity and a willingness to contribute and have fun that many people feel keep them in balance
all their lives. You won't find these qualities on any anatom-
ical chart, and there is no direct proof that they exist, other
than lots and lots of anecdotal evidence. But we know they
are there.

Your willingness to be human, to touch others in your life,
to be open to new experiences, to listen to and respond to
others, to learn from everything and everyone, to make
those around you laugh—all these qualities are keys to balance. Human touch is contagious and inspires others to live
balanced lives even as it affirms and maintains the life of its
originator. Why not let that originator be you?

# FIVE ZANY IDEAS FOR LIVING LIFE TO THE NTH DEGREE

We often forget or ignore our capacity to enhance our lives just by thinking and acting differently. We focus on worst-case scenarios and pessimistic projections. Yet some people insist that 90 percent of what we worry about never comes true anyway, so what are we trying to prove? If you're ready, then, to let go of negative airs that keep balance outside the door, try on a few zany, daffy insights that might actually welcome balance in.

## 1. The World Is Out to Help You!

Ever find yourself believing the opposite, that the world is out to get you? That's pretty easy to do, especially when Murphy's Law seems something like the Magna Carta. Some humor experts advise practicing "random acts of kindness." (You've seen the bumper sticker, perhaps?) Especially in the workplace, they say, kindness and helpfulness generate good vibrations that keep the atmosphere charged with plenty of positive, optimistic energy for all.

Specific suggestions: Hide a peppermint in the notes of that report your assistant's typing for you. When she gets to page 219, she'll appreciate the gesture! You can also show appreciation by sending a funny greeting card to colleagues or your supervisor, putting an inspirational saying on the company bulletin board, bringing along a banana pen or a quill to sign important documents at meetings. Just have some fun, for heaven's sakes!

The ice cream maker Ben and Jerry's, for example, offers its workers the opportunity to participate in the company "Joy Gang," an employee committee whose purpose is to spread joy and merriment to all company departments and stores.

Why not start your own joy gang?

## 2. Take a Break, Why Don't Ya?

Recent brain research indicates that taking mental and physical breaks from extended work periods refreshes people, helps them work out vexing problems, and gets them into a more productive frame of mind when they resume their concentration. Take breaks frequently! Don't be afraid people will think you're slacking off and not working very hard. You'll actually be working *harder,* or at least smarter, by keeping yourself sharp and performing at optimal mental and physical levels.

## 3. Say "Yes" to Yourself!

**Make sure you reward yourself not just for your victories, but even for just being you. If you acknowledge only your winning performances, you lose the opportunity to access the self-reward system at times when you may need it most.**

You're trying your best, aren't you? You're giving it all you've got, right? Then acknowledge these facts from time to time and give yourself a well-earned pat on the back. It's nice to hear an acknowledgment from someone else, too, of course, so if it doesn't come your way, do something really bold: Ask the other person for it!

One fabulous way to really acknowledge yourself is to give self-rewards from time to time. Did you finish a tough assignment last week? Go out and have that hot fudge sundae you never let yourself indulge in anymore. Forget worrying about eating all that fat—we're not gonna tell anybody. (In fact . . . we'll join you!)

One note of advice: Make sure you reward yourself not just for your victories, but even for just being you. If you acknowledge only your winning performances, you lose the opportunity to access the self-reward system at times when you may need it most. Keep up your spirits and your self-esteem any way you can. You're human. Say "Yes!" to yourself!

## 4. Program Your Brain Cells for Success!

A time-honored "positive thinking" technique for maintaining a positive attitude is the affirmation card. Write on an index card a statement of something you want, putting this statement in the form of a declarative sentence in the present tense with active verbs. Add superlative adjectives or adverbs.

Example: "I am exceeding my sales quotas every week with great gusto." Or: "I inspire my project team to excellent performances month after month." Or: "I am taking care of all my errands on weekends promptly and efficiently." Whatever you're after, say it in the most winning way.

Is this only some kookie New Age razzle-dazzle that sounds really nice and delicious but doesn't fit the real world? Uh-uh. You can actually program your brain with such simple techniques. Your brain gradually adopts each statement as truth, instructing your thinking processes to matter-of-factly find ways to implement them.

Carry your index cards around with you and read from them about fifteen to twenty times a day. Make out a card for every goal or desire you can think of. This simple, crazy idea really works! After a while, you won't be able to imagine doing things any other way than how you've put them on the card.

## 5.  Connect With Nature!

When you work (and live) so much indoors, it's easy to forget that a key aspect of who you are is your connection with nature. Since we humans have spent most of our millions of developmental years adapting to outdoor environments, it's only natural that true inner balance will be tough to achieve if you don't stay connected to the trees and the breeze.

When you take your breaks, when you acknowledge yourself for who you are, do so as much as possible outside. Find a quiet pond near your home or work, a garden path, an open field or city park, a favorite tree, or a slow country road. Some people swear that without access to a bucolic natural environment they could never ever experience true balance, no matter how powerful other techniques.

Keep your connection with nature an integral and ongoing segment of your schedule. Pencil it into your Day-Timer. You've got to have it.

## HOW TO DESTROY YOUR CREATIVITY

We all start out curious, creative, determined, willing. Don't believe us? Look no further than your children (or someone else's). If our eighteen-month-old Chloe Elizabeth wants to get closer to a remote control, she'll climb over every obstacle to get to it. She'll move lumbering coffee tables (she's the Schwarzenegger of the toddler set!), floor lamps, sofa beds, rocking chairs, and anything else that makes the mistake of sitting in her path.

Once there, she examines every molecule of the amazing, intricate device she holds now in her tiny hands. (Yes, time slows down for her—we've seen it!) And she stays with it until she's figured it out. Or at least until she's bored. Then it's on to the next adventure.

One eye-opening study we read about recently involves a test group of forty-five-year-olds who were measured for their capacities to be creative. Begun in the 1960s, this study found that only 2 percent of this age group could be considered highly creative, according to standards set by the researchers.

So the researchers decided to see what would happen if they moved their experiment down a notch. Testing forty-four-year-olds in exactly the same manner as the forty-five-year-olds, they found once again only 2 percent of the studied group could be entered into their "highly creative" category.

This got experimenters really curious, so they began moving their tests of the age groups downward. They tested forty-three-year-olds. Percentage scoring "highly creative"? Again only 2 percent.

Forty-two-year-olds were tested next. Again, 2 percent. Forty-one-year-olds, then all through the thirties and twenties and teens. Still 2 percent, each and every age group, all the way down.

When the researchers reached children aged seven, however, the percentage scoring "highly creative" finally changed. This time a whopping 10 percent made the grade. At age six, the percentage held at 10 percent, but at age five, inexplicably, the percentage scoring "highly creative" finally soared—to 92 percent!

What had happened? Why so low for so very long, and then suddenly, at a very young age, the completely opposite result? What explained the change?

It came to the testers all of a sudden. It was really so very, very obvious. Between the ages of five and eight, children begin attending school! Thus before we begin traditional learning, before we get funneled into what sometimes amounts to a big social conformity factory, we apparently function as purely creative beings.

What society values and teaches us at school gets reinforced at work and often, unfortunately, at home. Stagnation bombs, cloaked as realistic and practical tools for living, get lobbed at us all day long. They keep us stuck and stunted, not just personally but organizationally and societally as well.

Watch out for such stagnation bombs. You'll know when one hits you by the sinking feeling of dread that spreads immediately into your core. It stops you in your highly creative tracks, rendering you "same as everyone."

You'll recognize stagnation bombs at work by at least one of the following verbal warning signs:

- Forget about it! You're way ahead of your time.
- No one's ever going to buy that. They won't understand it.
- We've never done things that way before.
- We're not ready for that.
- Okay, fine. Now let's get back to reality.

- You'll be laughed right out of town with an idea like that.
- We've always done fine without it.
- That's not our problem.
- That's too far-out a change. No one will go for it.
- We've already tried that idea.
- It's a great idea but it'll never work.
- It's a great idea but we could never pull it off in time.
- You're not serious?
- Has anyone else ever tried this? We wouldn't want to be the first!

# CHAPTER 9

## THE END OF THE WIRE

The power of the visible is the invisible.

—Marianne Moore, American poet

We've illustrated in various ways throughout this book how the process of achieving balance is a journey. You never quite get there completely, but you feel yourself getting closer the more you try. Although life's tightrope will keep working to throw you off, if you stay focused on moving ahead (and not on falling), you can make it to the end of the wire. Then it'll be time to turn around and start back across again!

Constant course correction needs to take place, and continual reevaluation. How do you want things to be at this particular moment? How do you feel about your plans to get there? What changes do you need to make today in your Agenda of Desire and your Personal Balance Statement?

For a final review together, let's go back to your Personal Balance Statement, the one you compiled back in Chapter 1. In the time you've spent exploring balance since picking up this book, how have you changed? Does your Personal Balance Statement from Chapter 1 still accurately reflect how you want your life to be?

Take a moment to revise or flesh out your Personal Balance Statement. You might want to write out a brand-new one, if that suits you, or cross out a phrase here and there, or perhaps add a completely new dimension. Of course, it's okay too to just write out your Personal Balance Statement here exactly as you put it in Chapter 1, if you feel it's still pointing you in the right direction. You be the judge.

# UPDATED PERSONAL BALANCE STATEMENT

Now let's move on to an updated plan of action. Let's take a moment to consider any changes you need to make in the various areas we examined in this book. In fact, we'll review most of those areas and leave you room to add any we may have forgotten. Then, in the Breakthrough Solutions space that follows each review section, freewheel as many ideas as you can think of. You can write out your suggestions using full sentences, illustrate your suggestions, put together a collage in each space—whatever suits your fancy.

## FREEWHEELING BREAKTHROUGH SOLUTIONS

### Blocks I Need to Break Through

**1.** _____

**2.** _____

**3.** _____

**4.** _____

**5.** _____

### Breakthrough Solutions

## Communication Improvements I Need to Make

1. _____
2. _____
3. _____
4. _____
5. _____

## Breakthrough Solutions

## Time Issues I Need to Resolve

1. _____

2. _____

3. _____

4. _____

5. _____

## Breakthrough Solutions

## Flexibility Issues I Need to Improve

**1.** _____

**2.** _____

**3.** _____

**4.** _____

**5.** _____

## Breakthrough Solutions

## Miscellaneous Issues

1. _____
2. _____
3. _____
4. _____
5. _____

## Breakthrough Solutions

Now take the above Breakthrough Solutions and choose three from each category that you'd like to get started on now. Which three will help you make the most progress and resolve critical issues for you, blocks that just can't wait? Take care, though, to choose only three. Remember that you don't want to overwhelm yourself by taking on too much.

List all your top Breakthrough Solutions on a separate sheet of paper. Put each one in the format we described for your Agenda of Desire back in Chapter 3—first person, present tense, active verbs—and add a deadline to each. (Example: "I am supporting myself as a portrait painter by January 1, 1999.") When you're done, you'll have updated your original Agenda of Desire.

### Balance Check

- How does your Agenda of Desire now compare with the one you put together earlier?
- How have your needs changed?
- What goals have you achieved since putting together your original Agenda of Desire?
- Which blocks do you still need to work on?
- What desires have you now set for yourself that you hadn't considered before you picked up this book?

> **We're all capable at all times of achieving balance. No matter what the issue, dilemma, problem, or crisis, there's always a way out. Although our blocks work hard to convince us otherwise, we're all born with tremendous resilience, courage, determination, resourcefulness, and lots of other wonderful assets.**

We're all capable at all times of achieving balance. No matter what the issue, dilemma, problem, or crisis, there's always a way out. Although our blocks work hard to convince us otherwise, we're born with tremendous resilience, courage, determination, resourcefulness, and lots of other wonderful assets. These are the nuts and bolts of our "inner gyroscope," a self-correcting mechanism that signals us when we're straying off our course, then sets us back on track, and wakes us up when trouble comes snooping around again.

In balance one moment, out the next—by just listening to what's inside us we'll keep stepping gingerly across our personal tightropes. You are already in balance most of the time anyway, you know.

All you need do is acknowledge it.

# RESOURCES

Want to learn more about any of the issues we've explored in this book? We recommend the following books and resources with enthusiasm:

Alexander, Roy. *Commonsense Time Management.* New York: AMACOM, 1992.

Autrey, James A. *Life and Work: A Manager's Search for Meaning.* New York: William Morrow Publishers, 1994.

Bennis, Warren, and Burt Nanus. *Leaders.* New York: Harper & Row, 1985.

Bolles, Richard. *What Color Is Your Parachute?* Berkeley, Calif.: Ten Speed Press, 1994.

Carnegie, Dale. *How to Win Friends and Influence People.* New York: Simon & Schuster, 1988.

Covey, Stephen. *Seven Habits of Highly Effective People.* New York: Simon & Schuster, 1989.

Csikszentmihalyi, Mihaly. *Flow: The Psychology of Optimal Experience.* New York: Harper & Row, 1990.

Feynman, Richard P. *"Surely You're Joking, Mr. Feynman!": Adventures of a Curious Character.* New York: Bantam Books, 1985.

Garfield, Charles. *Peak Performers.* New York: William Morrow Publishers, 1986.

Grollman, Earl A., and Gerri L. Sweder. *The Working Parent Dilemma.* Boston: Beacon Press, 1986.

Hyatt, Carole, and Linda Gottlieb. *When Smart People Fail—Rebuilding Yourself for Success.* New York: Penguin Books, 1988.

Jeffers, Susan. *Feel the Fear and Do It Anyway.* New York: Fawcett Columbine, 1987.

McWilliams, Peter. *Do It! Let's Get Off Our Buts.* Los Angeles: Prelude Press, 1991.

———. *Life 101.* Los Angeles: Prelude Press, 1991.

———. *You Can't Afford the Luxury of a Negative Thought.* Los Angeles: Prelude Press, 1988.

Mayer, Jeffrey J. *If You Haven't Got the Time to Do It Right, When Will You Find the Time to Do It Over?* New York: Simon & Schuster, 1990.

Paulus, Trina. *Hope for the Flowers*. New York: Paulist Press, 1972.

Peters, Tom. *The Pursuit of Wow!* New York: Vintage Books, 1994.

Robinson, Bryan. *Overdoing It*. Deerfield Beach, Fla.: Health Communications, 1992.

Seligman, Martin. *Learned Optimism*. New York: Knopf, 1990.

Seuss, Dr. *Oh, the Places You'll Go!* New York: Random House, 1990.

Sher, Barbara, with Annie Gottlieb. *Wishcraft*. New York: Ballantine Books, 1979.

Sinetar, Marsha. *Do What You Love, the Money Will Follow*. New York: Dell Press, 1987.

Swiss, Deborah J., and Judith P. Walker. *Women and the Work/Family Dilemma*. New York: Wiley, 1993.

Wisinksi, Jerry. *Resolving Conflicts on the Job*. New York: AMACOM, 1993.